THE TIME WAS RIGHT

THE TIME WAS RIGHT

George A. E. Salstrand

BROADMAN PRESS
Nashville, Tennessee

Unless otherwise indicated, the Scripture quotations in this book are from the Revised Standard Version of the Bible. This version was copyrighted in 1946 and 1952 by the Division of Christian Education of the National Council of Churches and is used by permission.

Instead of using footnotes for quoted matter, the author's name appears in parentheses at the end of each passage. The Bibliography at the end of the book lists all sources used and quoted.

Library of Congress Catalog Card Number: 72–97604
Dewey Decimal Classification: 225.9
Printed in the United States of America

This book is dedicated
to my friend
Dr. Merrill C. Tenney
Dean of the Graduate School (1947–71)
Wheaton College, Wheaton, Illinois

Contents

Foreword

Doctrine may be written in different ways. It may be expounded in abstract teachings, precisely stating in theological terms the meaning of a great truth. This gives probably the most exact form of statement, and that is its great strength. Its weakness is that this form of statement may be static and frozen, far removed from life. The other way of setting forth doctrines is not to analyze them, but rather to exhibit them, to show instances or illustrations of them. Here the great strength is that the doctrine is in dynamic, dramatic form.

It is this latter type of book that Dr. George Salstrand has written. From the perspective of a theologian this book is a treatise on the doctrine of divine providence, although that is not what it is termed here. But it is a moving picture, not a still life. It is a narrative of God's preparation for the coming of the Savior. As such, it is a reminder that God is the sovereign Lord of mankind, of history, of all the universe. Here is a demonstration that God is alive and well. As one reads, he will be exposed to a considerable amount of biblical history, geography, and prophecy. He will find his mind challenged, but more than that, his heart will be warmed.

MILLARD J. ERICKSON, Ph.D.
Professor of Theology
Bethel Theological Seminary
St. Paul, Minnesota

Introduction

Stated in simple language, the providence of God has reference to the heavenly Father and his wise and benevolent provisions. As the good provider, God anticipated and took care of every need of his creation. Of most urgent concern was the need for redemption. Long ages before the birth of the Savior, the Divine Provider was actively preparing the world for this momentous event. This is the teaching of the apostle Paul as he states, "When the fulness of time was come, God sent forth his Son" (Gal. 4:4, KJV).

But what is the meaning of the expression "fulness of time"? Commenting upon this phrase as found in the Greek text of the New Testament, Vincent in his *Word Studies* says it refers to "the moment by which the whole pre-messianic period was completed." Then he further states that this expression means "plenitude of completeness" and "answers *to the time appointed of the father*" (Gal. 4:2, KJV).

Referring to the word "fulness" Zwemer says: "The Greek word . . . is *pleroma,* which means filled up to the brim. We know what it means in nature: first the blade, then the ear, and after that the fully ripened grain and the harvest. We know what it means in physics: you can saturate a solution up to the fulness of time and then it is no longer fluid, but crystalizes. We know what it means in physiology: the growth of the hidden ovum to maturity and birth, or the crisis in a fever. All these are illustrations of what we mean by the nick of time, the critical moment, the final process in a long series of events, all which have vital relation to each other and to the goal toward which they led" (p.-26).

History had been running its course for many millenniums. One civilization had been completely blotted out in the flood. Great world powers had arisen one after another—Egypt, Assyria, Babylon, Medo-Persia, Greece, and finally, Rome.

Three peoples of antiquity were outstanding in the contributions they made to civilization of the modern world. The first of these were the Jews. They gave the world monotheism in religion, the worship of the one God. The Greeks are also very important in civilization. They gave culture to the world, having produced some of the greatest thinkers of all time. The Romans are also very important. Their gift was jurisprudence with emphasis on law and order. The importance of the contributions of these three peoples is well stated by the New Testament scholar Dana who observed: "The world has found it best to worship with the Jew, govern with the Roman, and think with the Greek."

Aware that the Savior came into the world in the "fulness of time," my purpose of this book is to trace the providential preparations for the coming of the Savior in the histories of the Jews, the Greeks, and the Romans, and even in the geography of the land of Palestine.

Dr. Merrill C. Tenney was one of the lecturers when I made a tour of Palestine. I have dedicated the book to him because he gave of his valuable time to read the manuscript and make many helpful suggestions.

1. The New State of Judah
Remnant of Jewish Exiles Return to Build Homeland

As one opens the pages of the New Testament to the story of the life and ministry of our Lord as recorded in the Gospels, on almost every page appear references to individual Jews and companies of Jewish people. For this reason in order to understand the Gospels and the rest of the New Testament, it is essential to become acquainted with the origin and history of the Jews, especially the events related to this race in the five centuries preceding the birth of Jesus. The first four chapters of this book will deal with the history of the Chosen People during this important period of preparation for the advent of the Savior into the world.

I. Jewish Origins

The Jew represents a combination of elements contributed by the experiences of the many centuries of the past. He is, however, in a special way affected by the events of five centuries immediately preceding the birth of the Savior. From this period of history, we gain a knowledge of the origin and nature of the Jew.

H. E. Dana in *The New Testament World* says: "The Jew is strictly a distinctive character. The Israelite of the Old Testament may not be referred to correctly as a Jew. The Jew is a creation of the Exile, and appears in history at the time of the Restoration" (p. 66).

The word "Jew" is a modification of the tribal name Judah. The word first appears in the Bible in Esther 2:5. The book of Esther records events that occurred during the reign of King Ahazuerus (485–465 B.C.), who in secular history is known as Xerxes. As first used, the word "Jew" applied to Hebrews from Babylon who were usually from the tribe of Judah. Of the Jews, Josephus says, "This is the name they were called by from the day they came up from Babylon" (*Antiquities* 11:5).

The Jew occupied his ancient promised land, but Judaism grew up as something new on ancient soil. The terms "Jew" and "Judaism" have more than tribal significance. They refer to a distinct type of life. The Hebrews of the tribe of Judah who were carried captive had undergone a profound change. They were a repentant people. They recognized their privations in the Exile as the chastening hand of Jehovah because of their disobedience to the law.

Only the more devout Jews returned to their native land to reestablish the state of Judah as a holy nation. The descendants of Israel who returned from Babylon to Judah had a new devotion to the law and to the traditions of the fathers. They had a keen disgust for idolatry and for all things connected with Gentiles. Therefore, they were more intense and exclusive in their racial loyalty than their fathers had been before the Exile (Dana, *op. cit.,* p. 67). It was a renovated people who became known in history as the Jews.

II. The Babylonian Exile (597–539 B.C.)

In his book entitled *Biblical History of the Jews,* Foakes-Jackson says: "The captivity of Judah is one of the greatest events in the history of religion. . . . With the captivity the history of Israel ends and the history of the Jews begins" (p. 316). It was the capture of Jerusalem by Nebuchadnezzar, the king of Babylon, in the year 597 B.C. which brought to an end the first Jewish state. With this event the Babylonian Exile began.

It was during the course of the Exile that orthodox Judaism had its beginning. Many of those taken captive and transplanted to Babylon brought with them copies of the law and of the prophets which they cherished as their Scriptures. Although the sacrifice and the ritual of the Temple ceased, the worship of Jehovah continued. Some of the most devout and best educated Jews had been taken to Babylon, and with their settlement in the land sprang up a community which took the place of Jerusalem in religious leadership.

One of the important leaders of the Babylonian captives was the prophet Ezekiel who ministered to them twenty years. He predicted the restoration of the people to their land and foretold a renewal that would purify them from the abominations they had committed during the captivity (Ezek. 36:30–31).

Deprived of the ministrations of the Temple, each little community of Jews created its own meeting place. "Groups of the faithful banded together in the name of Jehovah, and formed congregations in which the law was taught and revered. Teachers were appointed who took the place of the Temple priesthood as religious leaders of the people. The study of the law took the place of animal sacrifices and ethical observances took the place of ritual" (Merrill C. Tenney, *New Testament Survey,* p. 51).

III. The Medo-Persian Period (539–333 B.C.)

With the fall of Babylon in 539 B.C., world sovereignty passed to the Medo-Persians. Cyrus, the new ruler of the Persian empire, was a benevolent despot. In dealing with conquered peoples, he reversed the cruel policy of the Assyrians and the Babylonians. The purpose of this section is to tell the story of the experiences of the Jewish remnant of exiles who in the Persian period returned to Jerusalem to rebuild their homeland, the Temple, and its worship ritual.

1. The First Migration (538 B.C.)

Recent findings indicate that Cyrus took Babylon in the fall of 539 B.C. During the first year of his reign Cyrus issued his decree giving the Jewish exiles in Babylon permission to return to their homeland. The decree encouraged the exiles staying in Babylonia to give offerings to the migrants. It also stated that the spoils of the Temple, which were confiscated by Nebuchadnezzar, would be returned.

The leader of the migration was Zerubbabel, whose Babylonian name was Shesh-bazzar, "the prince of Judah" (Ezra 1:8),[1] whom Cyrus appointed governor (5:14; cf. 2:2; 5:2,16). The associate of Zerubbabel (Shesh-bazzar) was Jeshua the high priest (2:2; 5:2). Some 5,400 sacred vessels from Solomon's Temple were returned to the Jews for use in the new Temple to be constructed (1:8–11).

The majority of the Jewish exiles did not return to Jerusalem. Already their roots were deep in Babylonia where they had built new homes and where they were enjoying prosperity. But almost 50,000 exiles, including servants and singers, made the long and dangerous one-thousand-mile trek from Babylon to Jerusalem.

After the migrants had arrived in Judah, they "gathered as one man to Jerusalem" (3:1) to begin construction on the Temple site.

---

[1] Some scholars look upon Shesh-bazzar and Zerubbabel as different persons. Bo Reicke in *The New Testament Era* says: "A few patricians and priests returned . . . under the leadership of a certain Shesh-bazzar, who is called a privy councillor for Jewish affairs (1:8,11; 5:15 f). This event is said to have provided the ground work for the later return under Zerubbabel" (p. 9).

Jeshua, the high priest, was in charge of the building operation, assisted by his fellow priests. So that they might reinstitute the offering of burnt sacrifices, the priests first built the altar of God which they erected on the old base (v. 3) and on the first day of October they offered the first "burnt offerings to the Lord" (v. 6). On October 15 the Feast of Tabernacles was again observed (v. 4).

The next phase of the building program of the Jews was the erection of the Temple. Again, Jeshua was in charge of the construction (vv. 8–11). But opposition from the natives around Jerusalem developed (4:1–6). As a result the work slowed and came to a halt (v. 24). During the next seventeen years, no more progress was made on building the Temple. But during that period the Jews were busy building houses for themselves (Hag. 1:4).

After the seventeen-year delay in rebuilding the Temple, the prophets Haggai and Zechariah urged that work be resumed (Ezra 5:1–2). When the local provincial officials (Persian satraps) saw the increased activity of the Jews, they asked, "Who gave you a decree to build this house and to finish this structure? (v. 3). The governor of Syria (v. 6) then sent a letter to King Darius, the new ruler of the Persian empire, asking if the Jews had been given permission to build the Temple and the city wall (vv. 7–10).

Upon receiving this inquiry, the king ordered a search of the government archives to see if authority had been given to the Jews to build the Temple. After the decree of Cyrus was found, the king commanded the provincial officials not to interfere with the construction of the Temple (6:7). He also ordered that the royal revenues of the province of Syria be given to the Jews to aid them in their building program (v. 8). In addition he instructed these officials to give the Jewish priests an adequate supply of animals for daily sacrifices. And he asked them to request the Jewish priests to intercede for the welfare of his reign (v. 9).

This meant that for the building of the Temple the Jews were given political support from the king and material aid by the district officials. From that time the work on the Temple proceeded at a rapid pace so that it was completed in the year 516 B.C. The new Temple was dedicated the same year (vv. 16–18). The Temple worship ritual was reactivated and the observance of the Passover was renewed (vv. 19–20).

The books of Ezra and Nehemiah give the only available information concerning the fortunes of the returned Jews and their new state of Judah. After the important events just treated, there is a long period of fifty-eight years on which we have no information. The book of Esther deals with that period, but it is concerned with the experiences of the Jews of the Exile under the Persian King Ahasuerus, or Xerxes.

2. The Second Migration (458 B.C.)

After the fifty-eight year period of silence, a second migration from Babylon to Jerusalem involving a new generation of Jews was led by the well-known scribe and priest whose name was Ezra. About eighteen hundred men and their families made this trek. The company consisted of Levites, singers, gate keepers, and Temple servants (Ezra 7:1–20). Without the protection of an armed guard, Ezra and his fellow travelers made the long and dangerous four-month journey from Babylon to Jerusalem.

The mission of Ezra was generously financed. The exiles who stayed in Babylonia gave free-will offerings for this project. More sacred vessels were carried back by the migrants for use in the new Temple. Moreover the king offered: "Whatever else is required for the house of your God, . . . you may provide it out of the king's treasury" (v. 20).

3. Nehemiah's Mission (445 B.C.)

Another dozen years pass in silence until in the year 445 B.C. a messenger by the name of Hanani and a few companions who had just returned from Jerusalem called on Nehemiah the Jewish cupbearer of the Persian King Artaxerxes.

As Hanani talked to Nehemiah, he told the king's cupbearer of the chaotic conditions he had found in Jerusalem. He reported that recently the walls of the city had been breached and the gates of the city had been burned. He also reported that the revival of Jewish political activities had provoked the native population of Palestine, especially the Samaritans.

The visitor's appeal fell on sympathetic ears. Nehemiah became troubled and brooded over what he had heard. King Artaxerxes noticed the sadness of his cupbearer and asked him for an explanation. In answer, Nehemiah frankly told the king the reason for his sadness and asked for a leave of absence from his position saying: "If it pleases the king, and if your servant has found favor in your sight, that you send me to Judah, to the city of my fathers' sepulchres, that I may rebuild it" (Neh. 2:5).

The result of Nehemiah's bold request was that the king authorized him to go on his mission. He also wrote letters introducing Nehemiah to the governors west of the Euphrates River asking them to supply him with building materials for the walls and the gates of the city, and for his own private home. Unlike the mission of Ezra, Nehemiah and his party were escorted to Jerusalem by the officers of the Persian army and cavalry. He went to Jerusalem with full authority to rebuild the walls of the city and to govern the Jews (Neh. 2:6–10).

After his arrival in Jerusalem, on the third night Nehemiah and a few of his trusted companions inspected the walls and gates of the city. It was to keep from arousing the suspicions of the hostile neighbors of the Jews that the inspection tour was made during the night.

After the inspection tour, Nehemiah reported to the inhabitants of Judah and challenged the Jews to begin building immediately. The wall was divided into sections. Each section was assigned to a different foreman and his crew. The workmen were assigned to work on the portion of the wall nearest their homes. All of the men of Judah were conscripted and were alternated between work shifts and guard duty. Thus, in spite of the opposition of the Samaritans, the walls and gates of the city were rebuilt in fifty-two days (vv. 15–16).

Having rebuilt the walls and the gates of Jerusalem, Nehemiah remained to govern Judah for twelve years. During this period a number of social reforms were enacted. One of the problems of the young state was that the money changers had been charging ruinous rates of interest. This practice was abolished (5:1–13). He also brought the public records up to date so that the descendants who had returned from the captivity might be known (7:5).

A remarkable experience of the Jews during the regime of Nehemiah was the renewal of the knowledge of the law under the leadership of Ezra the scribe. "Ezra had set his heart to study the law of the Lord, and to do it, and to teach his statutes and ordinances in Israel" (Ezra 7:10).

Through the thirteen years after his arrival in Jerusalem, Ezra had no doubt been gathering the Jews to teach them the law and to observe the various feasts and seasons. But with the walls of Jerusalem completed, the people had greater cause than ever to rejoice.

The Feast of Tabernacles was inaugurated in the sacred month of Tishri, the seventh month of the Jewish calendar, which in our calendar is October. The Feast of Tabernacles began the middle of the month and was observed for one week.

On this occasion as the people gathered in the square of the Water Gate, they requested Ezra to read to them the law of Moses and interpret it to them. In response to their request Ezra mounted a wooden platform and stood before the people to read the law as the Levites assisted in expounding it. It was an impressive service as Ezra assisted by the Levites "read from the book of the law of God, clearly" and as "they gave the sense, so that the people understood the reading" (Neh. 8:8). The result was a spiritual awakening as "the people wept when they heard the words of the law" (v. 9) and "they made confession and worshiped the Lord their God" (9:3).

After having governed Jerusalem for twelve years, in the year 432 B.C. Nehemiah returned to his position in the court of the Persian king, Artaxerxes. With the removal of his firm leadership, the period was characterized by laxness. One example is the case of Tobiah the Ammonite. When Nehemiah was leading the Jews in rebuilding the walls of Jerusalem, Tobiah did everything in his power to oppose. But when the governor left Jerusalem, Tobiah gained entrance to the city and moved into one of the chambers of the Temple. The room which he appropriated was the one that had been set aside as a storage place for the provisions of the Levites.

The people also neglected to bring in their daily offerings. And since the tithe of the offerings and of the firstfruits provided the major portion of the allowance of the Levites, they were forced to scatter through the countryside to earn a living from the land.

When Nehemiah returned to Jerusalem, he was indignant to learn that Tobiah, "the enemy of the Jews," had moved into the storage chamber of the Levites. But when Tobiah heard that the governor was back, he quickly vacated the chamber, which was renovated to again be used by the Levites (Neh. 13:4–9). And with Nehemiah's return, tithing was again instituted for the support of the priests and the Levites, with treasurers appointed to oversee the storehouses (vv. 10–13).

Mixed marriages had been a problem, both for Ezra and Nehemiah. Such marriages had been forbidden (Neh. 10:29–30). But during the later part of Nehemiah's governorship even one of the members of the high priestly family was guilty of disobedience of the law of intermarriage. Manasseh, a grandson of the high priest, had married the daughter of Sanballet, the governor of Samaria. Nehemiah excommunicated this priest, who, according to Josephus, fled to Samaria where he built the Samaritan temple with its rival worship on Mount Gerizim. Through this incident the bad relations between the Jews and the Samaritans became worse.

It was also near the close of Nehemiah's regime that Malachi uttered his prophecies. Being the last of the prophets, he had much to say about the messianic age. Like Nehemiah, Malachi also rebuked mixed marriages (2:11), and the withholding of the tithe (3:8–11).

Concluding Observations

The time involved in the Persian period was slightly more than two centuries (539–333 B.C.) of which Ezra and Nehemiah reported approximately one hundred years. It was during this period that the teaching of Moses was established as the basis of the national life of the Jews; that the first steps were taken in the formation of the Jewish canon of Scripture; that Jewish society was molded into a pattern that through the years has undergone very little change.

During this period also the Judea of the days of our Lord came into being; the rabbinic movement had its beginnings; and the Jewish attitude toward the Gentiles crystalized. In this period synagogue worship was developed; the sects arose which in Jesus' day were known as the Pharisees and the Sadducees; the priesthood became the supreme authority; also the strained relations between the Jews and the Samaritans developed into a serious schism.

2. Judah's Time of Trial
Hellenism and the Maccabean Revolt

After building the Temple and the walls of Jerusalem, the Jews enjoyed peace for approximately a century as they worshiped Jehovah and lived by the precepts of the Mosaic law. During that period their leaders were the priests and the scribes who regulated the minutest details of their lives. The Temple was the center of their existence. The Jewish state had gradually become a theocracy in which the priests and the law were supreme and in which the scribes were very influential.

But near the close of this long peaceful period, the basic beliefs and practices of the Jewish faith were suddenly endangered. This threat to Judaism was a result of the conquests of Alexander the Great and the introduction of Hellenism into the civilized world of that day.

The people of every conquered nation whether great or small were tempted to follow the popular gods of Hellenism. This contest was destined to continue for four centuries or until the destruction of the Jewish state in A.D. 70. During that period the Jewish nationalists fought a life-and-death battle against this new way of life. Jewish thought was influenced by this long struggle, but it survived distinct and more militant than ever. The purpose of this chapter is to trace this struggle through the Maccabean revolt.

25

I. The Rise of Hellenism

Of all the military leaders of history, one of the most brilliant was Alexander the Great. In a brief period of time, he conquered the Greek world and led his armies east to the borders of India.

It was in 334 B.C. when he was only twenty-two years old that Alexander struck his first blow in an attempt to overthrow the kingdom of Persia. In that year his forces dealt a crushing defeat to the western satraps of Darius III at the Granicus River. In 333 B.C. he pushed through southern Asia Minor to meet the Persian army under the personal direction of the emperor. The two armies fought at Issus and again the forces of Alexander were victorious. By this time fearful Darius offered terms of peace, saying that he would be willing to surrender all of his territory west of the Euphrates River. But Alexander refused. Then before pushing eastward, he planned to conquer the eastern ports of the Mediterranean Sea so as to bring about the collapse of the Persian fleet which was ruling the sea.

Alexander then attacked Damascus. After a quick victory he proceeded against Tyre, which yielded after a seven-month siege. After two more months Gaza was the next to fall. Before the end of 332 B.C., Alexander was the master of all Egypt. In this way he deprived the Persian fleet of its harbors and contact with its army. His next expedition was through Mesopotamia and Syria to the borders of India. By the time of his death at the age of thirty-three, Alexander was the master of the most impressive empire the world had ever known.

Alexander was an enthusiastic Hellenist. Wherever he went he found cities, beautified them with Greek art, and settled them with Greek colonists. In this way he introduced the language of Greece, her learning, coinage, and culture. Thus, he conquered not only the people but also their civilizations. This seed of Hellenism took root and continued to grow long after his death.

But Alexander did not train anyone to succeed him. Therefore, when he died in 323 B.C. his vast empire fell apart. Of the various generals who after Alexander's death divided his empire, two are important to this study. Ptolemy, who was one of Alexander's greatest generals, made himself the master of Egypt and established a dynasty which remained unbroken to the days of Caesar. The other was Seleucus, who, after fifty years of struggle, became the founder of the Seleucid Empire in Asia Minor, which extended from Armenia to Mesopotamia.

Judah as one of the smaller states of Palestine had a position between Egypt and Syria. Because the caravan routes to India and Arabia ran through Palestine, its territory was bitterly contested. During the period following the death of Alexander, with the struggle between Egypt and Syria going on, little Judah caught in the middle of the contest was like a ship in a storm, dashed by the waves from both sides. The little Jewish state passed from the one to the other of her powerful neighbors so that it was difficult to know which power to pay tribute to the next day. But because Jerusalem was located high on a mountain site, Judah was little affected by these changes. This was true because most of the military marches were along the maritime plain and through the plain of Esdraelon in Galilee. It must have been a relief, however, when in 198 B.C. the Seleucid dynasty established supremacy in Palestine.

In the years that followed, Hellenism made great strides in Palestine, which was encircled by Greek cities, and was continually under their influence. Sacrifices to the Greek gods were offered daily in the Philistine cities to the west and in the many temples along the Nile. Greek fashions, art, buildings, and sports were

common in the hamlets east of the Jordan River. Judah was bound
to be influenced. The big question was whether Judaism could
survive if Hellenism became dominant, or were the two spirits
mutually exclusive?

Concerning the Hebrew and Hellenic views of life with which
Judaism was confronted, Abram Leon Sachar in *A History of the
Jews* writes:

> The Hebrew stressed reliance upon an omnipotent God and conformity
> to a divinely sanctioned moral law; he was essentially serious, re-
> strained, willing to recognize his finite limitations. To seek God was
> the ultimate wisdom. His precepts the ultimate virtue. The Greek
> accepted no revelation as ultimate; he strove to penetrate to the core
> of his conceptions, analyzing the very basis of his knowledge. He was
> blessed with a delicate subtle reason and with a keen desire to use it,
> to probe with it and open the very heart of reality.
>
> The Hebrew was inclined to mysticism; he accepted the moral law
> and would not go beyond it. The Greek bowed to no law but that of
> complete self-expression. He loved beauty and art, the outdoor life, and
> every aspect of nature which appealed to his aesthetic sensibilities.
> Where the Hebrew asked, "What must I do?" the Greek asked: "Why
> must I do it?" . . . The uppermost idea with the Greek was to see
> things as they really are; the uppermost idea with the Hebrew was
> conduct and obedience. The Hebrew believed in the beauty of holiness,
> the Greek believed in the holiness of beauty (p. 100).

The two points of view cannot be reconciled in an individual.
"One could not accept a revealed law as ultimate, and yet question
the very foundations of life; or submit to a moral law and yet
exploit one's capacities without restraint" *(ibid.)*. But it might be
possible for both spirits to be present in a community with certain
individuals being good examples of each.

But unfortunately, the best of the Greek spirit did not meet the best in the Hebrew spirit. Instead there came to Judaism a degraded imitation of Hellenism. "Too often the gymnasium and the amphitheatre meant lewdness and licentiousness." Likewise, "The search for intellectual clarity meant dishonest banter and trickiness; the pursuit of the beautiful meant moral irresponsibility."

Coming after a long period of priestly sternness and puritanic piety, the Greek ideals wrought havoc in the Jewish state. At first only a few daring souls departed from the old ways. But as their number grew and as they became more bold, the older generation was shocked. The young people were shamelessly adopting Greek names and customs and were "displaying their nudeness in the Greek Palaestra." They attacked the laws and customs under which they had been reared. This was not merely a passing fad (*ibid.,* p. 101).

Two factions developed in the Jewish community. The one was the *Hasidim* or puritans. The other was the *Letzim* or Hellenists. They "filled the synagogues and the market places with their din as they sought to discredit each other." Judah was rent by two factions that could not understand each other. Almost every family was divided. "What was earnest to one group was jest to the other; what was pleasure to one was torment to the other. Those who loved Greek ways found Judaism crude and soul-depressing. The stern nationalists, on the other hand, drew no distinctions in judging the alien culture. Hating lasciviousness, they decried all that was beautiful in Greek art; hating sophistry and irreverence, they decried all that the philosophers taught. There was no compromise" *(ibid.)*

At first the victory seemed to go to the Hellenizers. They gathered to them the youth of all classes, including members of the aristocracy and the priests. Ambitious men who sought social advancement began living like Greek gentlemen. The old Judaism was in danger. But suddenly the Hellenists were thoroughly discredited, a reaction was brought about by the harshness and stupidity of a new Syrian monarch who had usurped the throne in 175 B.C.

II. The Threat of Syrian Hellenism

Palestine became subject to Syria in 198 B.C. With the transfer of Palestine to Syria came the rise of the Hellenistic party in Jerusalem. Under Syrian domination the Hellenists in Jerusalem increased in numbers and influence.

In 175 B.C. Antiochus IV succeeded to the Syrian throne. On his accession he adopted the surname Epiphanes, meaning "the manifest god," but because of his many foolish and horrible excesses, he soon earned the nickname Epimanes, meaning "the madman." He was an able despot and a thorough Hellenist. In his reign began one of the darkest periods of suffering in Jewish history, followed by glorious deliverance.

The accession of Antiochus as the emperor of Syria meant the triumph of the pro-Syrian party in Jerusalem. Previously no serious attempt had been made to Hellenize the Jews in Judah. But now all of this was changed. Onias IV who was the Jewish high priest had a brother by the name of Jason, who was the leader of the Hellenistic party in Jerusalem. This leader of the Hellenists by bribing the emperor succeeded in getting himself appointed as the high priest instead of his brother.

Having secured the appointment of high priest, Jason did his utmost to make Jerusalem another Hellenistic center like Antioch. Greek customs were introduced. The young men eagerly enrolled as citizens of Antioch. A gymnasium was erected in front of the military citadel guarding the Temple area. The youth of Judah competed with the Greeks in their games. Many of the young men submitted to an operation to remove the stigma of circumcision. They began wearing Greek clothes, especially the broad-brimmed Greek hat called the *petasos*.

In 171 B.C. a man by the name of Menelaus, who was also a Hellenizing Jew, was sent by the new high priest Jason on an errand to the Emperor Antiochus. While conferring with the emperor, he took advantage of the opportunity to offer him three hundred talents more for the high priestly office each year than Jason was paying. Unable to refuse such a generous offer, the emperor appointed Menelaus as the high priest instead of Jason. After his appointment, Menelaus raised the tribute money by taking it from the Temple treasury. This man who was thus elevated to the highest and most holy office in Judah was described by the writer of II Maccabees as one "who had the fury of a cruel tyrant, and the rage of a wild beast" (4:25).

The Hellenization of Jerusalem, which really meant its heathenization, now proceeded at a rapid pace. But reaction also set in so that many of the Jews became dissatisfied with their relation to Syria and wished that they were back under the rule of Egypt.

War broke out in 170 B.C. between Syria and Egypt over Palestine. By this time the sympathies of the majority of the Jews were with Egypt. And while these things were happening, a rumor came back to Jerusalem that Antiochus had been slain in battle. This led to great rejoicing in Jerusalem, and to a furious reaction. Though the new high priest Menelaus escaped, many of the Hellenizers were slain and for a short time the old regime was back in power.

But the rumor proved false. On his way back to Syria, Antiochus paid a visit to Jerusalem and learned what had happened. In anger he turned on those who dared to disregard his authority and restored Menelaus and his followers to their former positions. In

addition, being led by the wicked high priest, Antiochus entered
the Temple and into its holy of holies. And from the Temple he
carried away the golden altar of incense, the table of shewbread,
and even stripped the gold plating from the front of the Temple
(I Macc. 1:20–24; II Macc. 5:11–31).

Again in the spring of 168 B.C. Antiochus made another attack
on Egypt. The purpose was evidently to regain the city of Pelusium
on the eastern mouth of the Nile. But Egypt appealed to Rome,
the rapidly growing power of the west. The result was that Rome's
envoy ordered Antiochus to withdraw at once.

Frustrated by this turn of events, Antiochus determined to vent
his rage on Jerusalem where a strong pro-Egyptian party was now
active. He ordered his general Apollinus to Jerusalem with his
army of 22,000 men to wreak vengeance on the city. By talking
about peace, Apollinus and his soldiers were able to get into the
city, where he quartered his men until the sabbath. Knowing that
the Jews would not defend themselves on the sabbath, the Syrian
general waited for the day of worship and then released his men
on the helpless inhabitants of the city with instructions to slay
every man, and take the women and children captive to be sold
as slaves.

The orders of Antiochus were executed with relentless thorough-
ness. Jerusalem became a deserted city. The residents fled. The
walls were destroyed. The treasures of the Temple were stolen. The
daily sacrifice ceased to be offered. Drastic prohibitions were
enacted against Judaism. Sacrifice to Jehovah was ordered to cease;
sabbath observance was prohibited; circumcision was made a capital offense. The keeping of the sabbath and the reading of the law
were forbidden. All the sacred books that could be found were
confiscated and defaced.

But the most sacrilegious act was performed later. On December

15, 168 B.C., a heathen altar to Zeus Olympus was erected on top of the altar of sacrifice, and ten days later a hog was sacrificed, introducing the new heathen ritual "with all of its lascivious accompaniments." To devout Jews this was "the abomination of desolation" (I Macc. 1:54). Concerning Jerusalem, the Maccabean writer reporting these atrocities said: "Her sanctuary was laid waste like a wilderness; her feasts were turned into mourning; her sabbaths into reproach; her honor into contempt" (I Macc. 1:39).

III. The Maccabean Revolt

The bitter persecutions of Antiochus resulted in violent reaction among the Jews. The first effective resistance was initiated by an aged priest and his family in the village of Modin a short distance north of Jerusalem. The name of this priest was Mattathias. Because one of the ancestors of this priest bore the name Hasmon, his descendants are referred to as the Hasmonean line.

When one of the commissioners of Antiochus came blustering into Modin and asked Mattathias, as one of the most respected citizens of the city, to lead the way in offering a pagan sacrifice, the aged priest indignantly refused. And when a renegade Jew stepped forward and offered to make the sacrifice, Mattathias in righteous indignation killed the traitor and the commissioner as well. This was the spark that ignited the Maccabean revolt, which was destined to free Judah from foreign dominion for more than a century.

Mattathias and his five sons escaped to the mountains to raise the standard of revolt. The old man soon died, but before his death he committed the leadership of the revolt to his third son, Judas, who became one of the most impressive leaders of Jewish history. Judas soon earned the title Maccabeus which means "the hammerer." It was Judas who kindled the flames of patriotism and freedom in the hearts of his countrymen.

Judas became the captain of a little band of rebels who had no
training, no equipment, and little support, but they were men who
had learned to obey. Opposed to him were the best soldiers of the
east who were led by generals who had won fame in many battles.
Moreover the soldiers which they faced were far greater in numbers and were well-clad, well-trained, and well-armed.

The international situation, however, favored the Maccabean
rebels; for Antiochus was troubled by uprisings in the east, and
he could not concentrate on putting down the Jewish revolt. Large
numbers of the Syrian forces were committed to the prosecution
of the Parthian war.

Judas was a military genius and his soldiers fought like super-
men. Hiding with his men in the hills, Judas used the technique
of night attack to scatter the vastly larger armies of his Syrian
opponents. To Judas the Hasidim party rallied. The Hasidim were
the puritans who stood for a strict interpretation of the law.

Judas and his men won several important battles in rapid succes-
sion. One of these significant victories took place near Modin in
the narrow pass of Emmaus. When the Greeks came up this historic pass, Judas and his men attacked and sent the much larger
army of the Syrians fleeing toward the coast for their lives.

The next battle was at Mizpah where Judas triumphed enough
so that he was able to get control of the Temple. In 165 B.C. Judas
destroyed the pagan altars, cleansed the Temple thoroughly, and
amid the joyous praises of the people restored the worship of
Jehovah. The anniversary of this restoration is still celebrated in
Jewish homes as the Feast of Dedication.

Encouraged by these victories, Judas then dealt with some of
his lesser enemies. He pushed back the Idumeans and the Ammo-
nites so that by this time he was controlling a territory almost as

large as David's kingdom. But the warfare against the Syrians continued for years and in 161 B.C. while leading an army of only three thousand men against a much larger Syrian force, Judas was slain in battle. The place of Judas was taken by his younger brother, Jonathan, who in several battles inflicted severe losses to the Syrian forces, until by the treachery of the Syrian usurper Tryphon he was captured and executed.

After the death of Jonathan, the mantle of leadership of the Jews fell on the only remaining son of Mattathias whose name was Simon. In I Maccabees 14:41 we learn that Simon was declared by the Jews to be "their prince and high priest forever" or "until there shall arise a faithful prophet." In 142 B.C. Simon, the last of the five Maccabean brothers, was granted complete remission from tribute to Syria and was recognized as the high priest and leader of Judah. Simon and his descendants are usually thought of as the Hasmonean line of kings.

Concerning Simon, the writer of I Maccabees says: "The land had rest all the days of Simon, and he sought the good of the nation; and his authority and his glory was well pleasing to them all of his days. . . . They tilled their land in peace, and the land gave her increase, and the trees of the plains their fruit. . . . He provided victuals for the cities, and furnished them with all manner of munition, until the name of his glory was named unto the end of the earth" (14:4 ff).

Thus by an astounding combination of courage and good fortune, after centuries of servitude, the little state of Judah was once again independent. Many tears had been shed. Much blood had been spilled. But the faith of the people of Judah had been deepened by suffering and had been enriched by contact with new civilizations. Once again the little state had the opportunity to play a national role.

3. The Decline of Judah

How the Jewish State Became Roman Judea

The Maccabean brothers and their volunteer armies fought with great bravery for their faith. Finally after many bloody battles, Judah achieved the priceless privilege of liberty to worship Jehovah according to the directions of the Torah.

Having attained this liberty, the Hasmonean rulers (descendants of the Maccabees) were not content with their heritage but sought to enlarge their borders. These priestly rulers engaged mercenary armies which they led in the conquest of their surrounding neighbors. Moreover, the people of the conquered tribes were forced to become nominal Jews by the rite of circumcision.

This chapter begins with the record of a high peak of material prosperity. Simon, the last of the Maccabean brothers, became the first ruler of what came to be known as the Hasmonean line of kings of Judah. This prosperity continued through the thirty-year reign of John Hyrcanus, the son of Simon. But during the reign of Hyrcanus, there was a growing discontent with the image of the high priest leading mercenary armies. With the short reign of Aristobulus, the twenty-six-year regime of Jannaeus, and the nine-year rule of Alexandra, there was a period of discontent and decline which ended in civil warfare. Finally, the armies of two high priestly claimants to the throne battled for supremacy.

During this period political events in Judah went from bad to worse. Finally, an Idumean named Antipater, through his plottings and manipulations, was able to bring about the downfall of the Hasmonean line of kings. Then, after Antipater's death, his son Herod was appointed by the Roman emperor as the king of the Jews. Such is a brief preview of the sad but fascinating story of this chapter.

I. The Decline of Maccabean Judah

1. The Reign of Simon

Simon who was the ablest of the Hasmoneans was a splendid ruler during the period of Judah's reconstruction. Although Simon combined civil and military leadership with his office of high priest and although he had all the substance of regal authority, he refrained from calling himself king.

After several attempts, the forces of Simon captured the citadel of Akra which overlooked the Temple, thus freeing the Jews from the menace of a foreign garrison in their midst. He also captured the coastal cities of Gazara and Joppa and through these cities a brisk business in foreign trade developed. And in addition to his other accomplishments, he also negotiated a treaty with Rome.

But the reign of Simon was brought to a sudden and tragic end when he and his two old sons were assassinated by his son-in-law Ptolemy who planned to usurp the throne. But the evil plan miscarried. John Hyrcanus the youngest son of Simon learned about the plot in time to refuse the invitation to the dinner where the assassinations were to take place and thus escaped.

2. The Reign of John Hyrcanus

When the news of the slaying of his father and brothers came to him, Hyrcanus immediately set out for Jerusalem to claim his inheritance, arriving before Ptolemy.

John Hyrcanus was destined to rule Judah for thirty years. He threw off the Syrian yoke and made an alliance with Rome. He created a mercenary army and sought to play a role of leadership in the Mediterranean world. He subjugated the Idumeans in southern Palestine who had given Judah considerable trouble. He offered the Idumeans the alternative of exile or circumcision. They chose circumcision and thus became nominal Jews. He also subjugated the Samaritans and destroyed their rival temple on Mount Gerizim. He was the first Jewish ruler to have his name stamped on the coins of his state. Under Hyrcanus Judah reached the peak of her prosperity.

Trouble was brewing. The simple piety and religious ferver of Mattathias had given way to desire for conquest and glory. But the sight of the high priest leading armies of mercenary soldiers must have caused concern to the Hasidim, or the pious Jews that composed this party. For Hyrcanus all desire for humble sacrifice to Jehovah was gone. For him the office of high priest was only a political position.

On one occasion to allay opposition, Hyrcanus gave a dinner for the leaders of the state. Among those invited were certain members of the Hasidim, later known as the Pharisees. After the dinner Hyrcanus asked his guests for criticisms of his rule. At first everyone flattered him. But a certain Pharisee by the name of Eleazer suggested that he ought to resign the office of high priest and confine himself to the affairs of civil government. When pressed for an explanation of his suggestion, Eleazer replied that it was noised about that the mother of Hyrcanus had been a captive during the reign of Antiochus Epiphanes, which intimated that the paternity of Hyrcanus was uncertain thus making him ineligible for the office of high priest.

This insinuation of Eleazer so greatly angered Hyrcanus that he demanded that the Pharisees punish the offender. When the Pharisees decreed a rather mild punishment of "stripes and bonds," Hyrcanus was outraged and broke his fellowship with them, declaring himself to be in sympathy with the Hellenistic party represented by the Sadducees.

Thus, during this period the political aspirations of the high priest rulers of Judah were arousing fears and discontent. When Hyrcanus thus broke with the Hasidim, it was an indication that "the last vestige of patriotism vanished from the Maccabean family." With the death of Hyrcanus, the glory of the Hasmonean line of rulers declined.

3. The Short Reign of Aristobulus

The next Maccabean ruler was Aristobulus. It appears that Hyrcanus intended for Aristobulus to succeed him only as high priest since he had designated his wife to administer the government. But immediately after the death of his father, Aristobulus had his mother and brothers imprisoned and assumed full control over Palestine. He followed his father's example in pushing conquests through Galilee. He went a step further than his father when he actually had himself crowned king. And like an oriental king he even destroyed the members of his own family whom he thought were a threat to his throne.

4. The Reign of Alexander Jannaeus

After the death of Aristobulus, his childless widow released his brothers from prison and married the oldest, whose name was Alexander Jannaeus. At the time of the wedding he was twenty-four and she was thirty-seven. Thus in 104 B.C. both the civil and the religious powers were in the hands of "the capable and ruthless young grandnephew of Judas Maccabee."

Jannaeus was a warrior. He began his twenty-six-year reign by murdering his brothers. He devoted much time to extending his territory. He proceeded to conquer Galilee and the territory east of the Jordan. As the years passed, opposition against him grew in violence.

There was increasing dissatisfaction with having a high priest whose main interest was in leading mercenary armies rather than "in humble adoration of the true king." Moreover Jannaeus was not very successful as a warrior. For example, on one occasion his forces followed an Arabian chieftain into a ravine. There they found themselves hemmed in on all sides. The enemy then drove camels over the company so that nearly all were trampled to death.

Another story tells that one year during the celebration of the Feast of Tabernacles as Jannaeus was officiating as high priest at the altar, his enemies began "pelting" him with lemons. Josephus records that in revenge Jannaeus had some six thousand of his subjects executed. Then for six years Jerusalem was the scene of civil war.

On another occasion Jannaeus is said to have asked the Pharisees what he could do to please them. Their arrogant reply was that he could kill himself. As the result of this opposition by the Pharisees, Jannaeus took bitter vengeance on them, crucifying eight hundred of them, while before their eyes he massacred their wives and children.

It was Jannaeus who appointed Antipas as the governor of Idumea which had been conquered by his father. It was the son of Antipas, whose name was Antipater, who later played an important role in the history of the Jews.

5. The Reign of Alexandra

After the death of Jannaeus in the battle of Ragaba, east of the Jordan, Alexandra his widow succeeded to the throne. Evidently seeing that it was futile to oppose the Pharisees, Alexandra cast her lot with them and raised them to power. She made her brother Simon ben-Shetach the prime minister, and from Alexandria she called in another able Jew named Judah ben-Tabbai. These men were both ardent Pharisees who initiated sweeping reforms. Under their influence Alexandra gave more authority to the local council of Jerusalem so that in addition to the nobles and the priests who previously constituted the council, the queen introduced a new group, namely, the scribes.

The queen's brother ben-Shetach seems to have been her confidant. In all phases of her government the power of the Pharisees was in evidence. In three succinct statements the Jewish historian summarized the relation of the Pharisees to the queen. On one occasion he stated, "while she governed other people . . . the Pharisees governed her." Another time he said: "So she had the name of Regent; but the Pharisees had the authority." On a third occasion he recorded: "The Pharisees have the multitude on their side." Thus, during the nine-year reign of Queen Alexandra the Pharisees won a place of supremacy in the government of Judah which they retained to the time of Jesus when they constituted the leading Jewish party.

Being a woman, Alexandra was ineligible to officiate as high priest; therefore, she appointed to this office her weak and incompetent son Hyrcanus II. But because her younger son Aristobulus II was a threat to the throne, he was kept from a position of power, though on occasion he was used as a general. Thus he was forced to await the right moment to seize the reigns of government.

The fatal illness of Alexandra became the opportune time for Aristobulus. After the death of Alexandra, Hyrcanus was in nominal command. But the disgruntled nobles who were now strategically placed throughout Palestine gave their ready support to Aristobulus. Overnight he became a menacing figure. Hyrcanus was no match for his brother and his forces were quickly defeated in a battle near Jericho. Thus Hyrcanus was deprived of his twofold position of priest and king. He then quite peacefully accepted this turn of events and retired from public life to live in the former house of Aristobulus while his energetic younger brother took over the palace as his residence.

The stage was set for the series of events which would result in the overthrow of the Hasmonean dynasty and the entrance of Rome into the affairs of Palestine.

II. Palestine Under Roman Rule

Up to the time of its contact with Hellenism, the Jewish state was known as Judah. But after the Hellenization of Palestine, Judah became known as Judea, as pronounced in Greek.

It will be remembered that John Hyrcanus conquered the Idumeans and forced them to become nominal Jews by circumcision. Years later his son Jannaeus appointed Antipas, a native of Idumea, as the governor of that territory. Still later Antipater, the son of Antipas, succeeded to his father's command. The new governor of Idumea and later the Roman procurator of Palestine, through plots and manipulations exercised a directing influence in Judea. He operated as the power behind the throne of Hyrcanus, whose interests he pretended to be serving. The political activities of Antipater brought about the fall of the Hasmonean dynasty and finally after his death the crowning of his own son Herod as the king of the Jews.

When Aristobulus gained the victory over the forces of Hyrcanus, Antipater felt the time was ripe for intervention. Realizing that Hyrcanus would be easier to control than his younger brother, Antipater sought to prod Hyrcanus into action. This he did by persuading him that his brother Aristobulus was plotting his death. He then persuaded Hyrcanus to flee to Petra, the capital city of Aretus, the Arabian chieftain, from whom he had received a promise of assistance.

When Hyrcanus arrived at Petra, Antipater convinced him that he should try to regain his lost position. Aretus promised Hyrcanus aid, provided the twelve cities which had been taken from him by Jannaeus be returned. With such strong support from the Arabians, the forces of Aristobulus were soon put to flight. When many of his followers deserted, Aristobulus retreated to Jerusalem where he could count on the support of the priests. There he took refuge in the Temple.

Pompey's general Scaurus was at this time in Damascus. He saw in the civil war of the two brother priest-king claimants to the throne of Judea an opportunity to intervene on behalf of Rome. Upon his arrival in Judea, both sides made overtures to him. He decided to disperse the Arabians. He did this by ordering them to leave the city of Jerusalem or suffer the wrath of Rome. With the Arabians gone, Aristobulus was temporarily reinstated to his position, pending the arrival of Pompey.

There was no further change during the next two years. But when Pompey arrived in Damascus to make arrangements for the administration of Palestine, both brothers appealed to him. In addition, there was a third appeal by a committee of Jews that did not want either of the brothers but asked for the restoration of the rule of the priests. This request voiced the dissatisfaction with the later Hasmoneans who as priest-kings had also been fighters.

Upon hearing the various arguments, Pompey sent the contending parties away, promising that on his arrival in Palestine he would deal with their problems. But Aristobulus angered Pompey by leaving him at Dium, where he had accompanied the Roman legions, to hurry to Alexandria. This created a crisis. Immediately the Roman general marched his legions into Palestine and to Jerusalem. When Aristobulus saw the Roman soldiers just outside of Jerusalem, he promised to open the gates and surrender the city. But when Pompey sent his emissaries to receive the city, they found it ready for resistance. He immediately arrested Aristobulus and besieged the city, and through the aid of the followers of Hyrcanus he took the city without bloodshed. However, the forces of Aristobulus retreated to the stronghold on the Temple mount. After a three-month siege in which some twelve thousand Jews were killed, the stronghold was finally taken. Upon his capture of Jerusalem, Pompey appointed Hyrcanus the high priest and ethnarch of Judea.

Thus the independence of Palestine came to an end, and although Hyrcanus was given the title of high priest and ethnarch, he no longer had the title of king and he was responsible to Rome. Moreover, the territory of the Jews was greatly diminished in size. The important seacoast towns were taken away and were given to Syria. Samaria and many Hellenistic towns in Galilee and east of the Jordan were set free from the hated Jewish yoke. Judea was no longer a kingdom.

But with Palestine under Roman jurisdiction, Judaism became one of the recognized religions of the empire. The Jews were allowed their own judicial and legislative body in the Sanhedrin which had jurisdiction over civil and minor offenses. For some years there was peace and prosperity and the Jews were well treated by the Romans.

An interesting chain of events now begins which was to result in the appointment of Idumean Herod as the king of the Jews. Antipater again comes into the picture as a cunning, ambitious, and resourceful leader. In the war between Hyrcanus and Aristobulus, he espoused the cause of the weaker Hyrcanus who, because of his backing, won the position of high priest and ethnarch. In this struggle Antipater succeeded in making himself indispensable both to Hyrcanus and to the Romans so that Julius Caesar appointed him procurator of Palestine. Then as the procurator of Palestine, Antipater appointed his son Phasael as the governor of Judea and his other son Herod as the governor of Galilee. Having accomplished these strategic goals, he himself was poisoned by a fanatical Jew.

Herod's early career was marked by a struggle for supremacy. The death of his father Antipater left him the governor of Galilee while Herod's brother was the governor of Judea. Then Julius Caesar was assassinated and his brother Phasael committed suicide. But Herod succeeded in evading his enemies and after much difficulty reached Rome. When he arrived in 40 B.C., Antony and Octavian who were now friends were engaged in parcelling out the Roman world. And because they recognized his ability, Herod succeeded in enlisting their aid. Within seven days of his arrival in Rome, he left the capital city having received the title king of the Jews. Then returning to Palestine with a small armed force and gathering more support as he proceeded, Herod captured Jerusalem in 37 B.C.

Having obtained his objective, Herod immediately proceeded to rid himself of all his opponents. Antigonus, who was the son of Aristobulus II and who had aspired to the throne, was executed along with all but two of the seventy members of the Sanhedrin. Later the fair young Aristobulus, whom Herod had appointed under pressure to be high priest, was drowned. The drowning was said to be accidental, but it was common knowledge that the young priest was too popular with the people. Even the aged Hyrcanus who by this time had reached seventy-five years and had long been the tool of Herod's father's ambition was the next to be executed. Also Mariamne who was a Hasmonean and the most beautiful and beloved of Herod's wives was accused of unfaithfulness by Herod's sister Salome and was condemned to die. Her fate was also repeated in the execution of her "proud and sagacious mother."

But Herod's early career in bloodshed now gave way to a real effort to become a progressive administrator. Having disposed of all who might be a threat to his right to the throne, Herod turned his attention to the improvement of his kingdom. He became an enthusiastic patron of culture and art. He entered upon a tremendous campaign of reconstruction in which he demonstrated real administrative ability. He built a magnificent port to accommodate the ships of the nations and the port city of Caesarea, which he named after his patron. He improved and enlarged Samaria and renamed it Sebaste, which means Augustus, in honor of the Roman emperor. He built many forts and defenses and did the job so well that some of them remain to the present time.

He rebuilt the Temple in Jerusalem with even greater magnificence than the Temple of Solomon. With its white marble overlaid with gold and precious stones, it gleamed in the sunlight as it stood high on Mount Zion. As the pilgrims journeyed up the Jericho road and over the Mount of Olives, this beautiful sight burst into view with all of its magnificence so that it gave rise to the familiar rabbinical statement: "Whoever has not seen the Temple of Herod has seen nothing beautiful." The Temple was to be the crown of Herod's realm and he had hoped that it would make Jews feel more kindly toward him.

Herod, however, did not die in peace. His reign closed in a state of domestic chaos. He never recovered from the execution of Mariamne, who was his favorite wife and the only woman he ever loved. Remorse preyed on his conscience and he became insanely morose. When they were of proper age, he sent his sons Alexander and Aristobulus to Rome to be educated. These splendid looking young men were the sons of Mariamne. They were the descendants of the famous Hasmonean family and were designated as Herod's heirs. But when they returned from their training in Rome, they proved so popular that Herod accused them of plotting to seize the throne and had them executed as well. Later he learned that another son, Antipater, was devising a plot against his life, for which he also was executed. Such was the background when "wise men from the east came to Jerusalem," asking, "Where is he who has been born king of the Jews?" (Matt. 2:2). It is no wonder that the sacred writer records: "When Herod the king heard this, he was troubled, and all Jerusalem with him" (v. 3). The slaughter of the innocents which followed fits perfectly into this pattern of suspicion and cruelty.

In accordance with Herod's will which he made a short time before his death, his three ~~~~~~ ame into possession of his realm when he died in 4 ~.~. Archaelaus was made the king of Judea, which included Palestine and Idumea. Herod Antipas became the tetrarch of Galilee and Perea, and Herod Philip became tetrarch of Trachonitis and adjacent regions.

4. The Jews of the Dispersion
The Extent and Meaning of the Diaspora

In the preceding chapters, attention was centered on the Jews of the Babylonian captivity, who, during the Persian period, returned to rebuild the Temple and the walls of their city and to reestablish the state of Judah. The history of these Jews and their descendants was traced from the time of the Babylonian captivity to the time of Christ.

But there were also descendants of the Northern Kingdom of Israel who were taken captive when Samaria the capital fell to the Assyrians in 722 B.C. These captives never did return to their homeland. This was also true of the great majority of the Jews who were deported to Babylon. As things worked out, most of the Jews who elected to remain in the lands of their exile were scattered throughout the civilized world by the time of Christ.

These Jews who were scattered among the nations came to be known as the *Diaspora*, the Greek term meaning dispersion or scattering. This term was used to designate Jews living in both small and large communities outside of Palestine and more especially beyond the borders of Judah. It described the relation of Jews to the many countries in which they settled. These Jews on the one hand made regular contacts with their mother country, and on the other hand were in touch daily with the Gentile world. They became of great importance to the internal development of Judaism and its influence on the civilized world.

I. Some Biblical References to the Dispersion

Moses had predicted a dispersion of the children of Israel in the event they abandoned the law (Lev. 9:3; Deut. 4:27–28; 28:64–68; 30:1). The scattering as a punishment for disobedience also found frequent expression in the prophets (Hos. 9:3; Jer. 8:3; 16:15; Ezek. 4:13; Zech. 10:9). That the dispersion of the Jews was to benefit the Gentiles is alluded to in Psalm 67 and in Micah 5:7.

In the Fourth Gospel, John referred to the Dispersion. He quoted Jesus as saying: "You will seek me and you will not find me; where I am ye cannot come" (7:34). Then as the puzzled Jews pondered Jesus' statement, they asked one another, "Where does this man intend to go that we shall not find him? Does he intend to go to the Dispersion among the Greeks and teach the Greeks?" (v. 35).

Though Luke did not mention the term, he alluded to the Dispersion when he listed the various provinces of the Roman Empire from which those present at the Feast of Pentecost in Jerusalem had come (Acts 2:9–11).

II. A Historical Sketch of the Dispersion

The causes of the Dispersion were varied. In connection with the Assyrian and Babylonian captivities, the conquerors of the ten tribes of Israel and the two tribes of Judah deported large masses of the nation of Israel into their eastern provinces. Many of the best families of Israel and Judah never returned to their homeland but settled in the lands to which they had been brought. In these lands they developed industries, and under the leadership of such men as Ezekiel and Ezra, they organized the old tenets of their faith into forms that spread far and wide. From Babylonia, Jews of the Dispersion found their way over the ancient trade routes into Media, Persia, Egypt, Cappadocia, Armenia, and Pontus.

When Alexander the Great came on the scene, the Jews began to go west. His conquests turned dangerous trails into safe and open highways of trade which many of the Jews hastened to use. Strabo spoke of the scattering of the Jews during this period saying: "Now these Jews are already gotten into all cities; and it is hard to find a place in the habitable earth that hath not admitted this tribe of men, and is not possessed by them."

Syria and Asia Minor contained many more Jews than Palestine itself. This was because of the intimate though not always pleasant associations between Palestine and the Seleucid empire which resulted in large migrations to the north. The capital city Antioch had a sizable Jewish community.

Also from the Jewish centers of Mesopotamia and Babylon, Antiochus the Great of Syria removed some two thousand families and settled them in Phrygia and Lydia. Many Jews also voluntarily emigrated to Asia Minor, especially to the towns of the Ionic Coast and the more important ports and commercial cities of the Mediterranean Sea. In Asia Minor such cities as Antioch in Pisidia, Iconium, and Ephesus all had Jewish communities. This was also true of the Greek cities of Thessalonica, Corinth, and Athens.

In 139–138 B.C. the Roman senate sent out a circular letter in favor of the Jews to the kings of Egypt, Syria, Pergamos, Cappadocia, Parthia, and a great number of provinces and towns in the Mediterranean Sea (I Macc. 15:16–24).

Alexandria in Egypt was one of the many Hellenistic centers. In it Greek learning flourished and to it multitudes of Jews migrated. To this great city, linking the east and the west, so many Jews came that by the time of the birth of Christ the Jewish community is estimated to have numbered well over a million. It is likely that it was to this Jewish community that Joseph and Mary fled with the infant Jesus to escape the wrath of Herod the Great.

After the death of Alexander, Egypt was ruled by the Ptolemies until conquered by Rome. The Ptolemies were good rulers and they succeeded in making their capital city Alexandria the center of intellectual and economic life in the world of that day. The famed museum with its chapels, halls, and libraries has been described as "the prototype of our college foundations." The library was one of the wonders of the world. At the time of the death of Ptolemy Philadelphus, it contained some 100,000 rolls. Each emperor added to the collection until it reached a total of more than 700,000 rolls. But in the siege of Julius Caesar in 47 B.C., it was destroyed by fire. However, it was reestablished and again achieved fame only to be destroyed once more in A.D. 640 by the Muhammadan conqueror Caliph Omar.

In Alexandria we get the clearest picture of the change that came into Judaism as the result of the residence of the Jews of the Dispersion in an alien but friendly atmosphere. In this great city the Jews lived as honored citizens. Not only in the Jewish quarters, but throughout the city their synagogues were to be found and some of them were very large.

In this cultural center of Alexandria which was for the most part free from persecution, the Jewish citizens assimilated the alien culture and philosophy of the Greeks, and Alexandrian Judaism contributed to the life and thought of the day through the literature which it produced.

The Greek culture which had greatly affected the inhabitants of Alexandria also affected the Jews. From the days of Alexander the Great, Greek became not only the language of culture, but of business as well. Although the Jews of the Dispersion retained their religious loyalty and ceremonial observances, and though Jerusalem remained their mother city, it was impossible for the Jews who spent their lives in the business world of the Greek cities like Alexandria to retain the use of their Semitic language. So the Jews of the Dispersion adopted the language used in their business transactions, namely, Greek. It was not classical Greek, however, but the language of "the street patois," a strange conglomeration of many alien elements.

III. Synagogue Worship in the Dispersion

The word "synagogue" is the translation of the Greek word *synagoge* which means "a gathering of the people" or a congregation. It has reference to a Jewish religious community or sanctuary.

Little is known about the origin of synagogue worship, but it seems to date back to about the sixth century B.C. or the Babylonian captivity when the Jews were separated from the Temple, the only place where sacrifices might be offered. It is believed that it was about the time of the Exile that the Jews began to meet in local groups to study the Pentateuch in order to fulfil the ancient law. As a place of instruction and prayer, the synagogue may have originated in such meetings.

While the word "synagogue" is not mentioned in the Old Testament, some scholars think that the story of Ezra reading from the law (Neh. 8) was inspired by the synagogue practice of that day. If so, this is our earliest source of information on the subject.

When we turn to the New Testament, we find more than fifty references to synagogues either as communities of persons organized for religious purposes, or as buildings in which gatherings for such purposes were held.

The rapid grouth of synagogues after the Exile can be attributed to the fact that they were places where the law was read and studied. It was the conviction of Israel that her hopes would not be realized until they lived in accordance with God's law as revealed in the sacred Scriptures. This made it necessary to teach this Divine revelation to all Jews.

Judaism is a religion in which knowledge is imperative. God had revealed his will to men and they must know his will in order to do it. Thus, the synagogues became the "rallying points" of Judaism. Philo spoke of the synagogues as "houses of instruction." In addition to the services on the sabbath, the Jews met in their synagogues twice each week for the study of the Scriptures and for prayer.

In the synagogue service selections from the law were read. As time went on the Pentateuch was divided into readings that might be completed in three years. Then later, following the Babylonian practice, these readings were arranged in such a way that they could be completed in a year. These Scripture portions were first read to the congregation in Hebrew and then were translated into the current Aramaic. Eventually these "rough-and-ready" paraphrases were reduced to writing and became known as Targums.

These synagogues had no fixed ministry. Any qualified person might be invited to read the text, translate, or speak. Scholars who were members of the congregation or who were visitors might be invited to speak. This is illustrated in the New Testament when on one occasion Jesus was invited to speak in the synagogue of Nazareth. Having read the lesson from the scroll of Isaiah, Jesus handed it back to the attendant and sat down to expound it (Luke 4:16–22). Again in the synagogue of Antioch in Pisidia, the rulers invited Paul and Barnabas to speak saying: "Brethren, if you have any word of exhortation for the people, say it" (Acts 13:15–16). Again in the synagogue of Thessalonia, Paul "as was his custom . . . argued with them from the scriptures, explaining and proving that it was necessary for the Christ to suffer and to rise from the dead" (Acts 17:2–3).

Angus in his book entitled *The Environment of Early Christianity* informs us concerning this unique institution saying: "The synagogues became to each town what Judea was to the world. It was to the heathen a school of morals and religion. It became the cradle of Christianity. As the Temple service passed more definitely under the control of the aristocracy, the synagogue grew in influence with the masses, it was the meeting place of the people with their teachers. There they heard the Law and the Prophets; there the hope of Israel was kept green. When the Temple was finally destroyed, the synagogue became all in all to Israel. Wherever ten males were found in a town a synagogue was formed" (p. 151).

These synagogues which were very numerous were usually erected on the most favored locations in each city. It was around these synagogues that the Jews carried on their proselyting work. The Jews who were members of these synagogues which were spread throughout the Graeco-Roman Empire were the first missionaries and preachers. They believed that in Abraham and his seed all the nations of the world were to be blessed. They believed that the God of Israel should be called the God of the whole earth, and that Israel should have a prominent place as a medium of better things for the race.

The influence of the many synagogues was not in vain. Conversions to Judaism were frequent. In spite of the fact that the Jew was usually despised, the serious heathen could not be indifferent to the attraction of his moral life. Angus observes: "We can scarcely imagine how refreshing these services of prayer and exhortation must have been to the heathen who lived in a world that felt the burden of the age and on whom were settling a boredom and a weariness, whose golden age lay behind them. They came into contact with a people who were continually renewing their youth, and whose golden age and brightest hopes lay in the future" (*ibid.*, pp. 153–54). It was by the synagogue that the Jew taught the ancient world to pray, both by example and precept.

Schurer attributes the success of Jewish propaganda through the synagogue to three causes. He felt that in the synagogue Judaism presented its best aspect to the pagan world. The Jews in their synagogues dropped all that was offensive and did not emphasize that which was unimportant or exclusive. Rather, they laid emphasis on what would receive a sympathetic hearing, such as their lofty idea of God, and the authority of a religion of revelation. Their practical aim was a moral and happy life. Moreover, the trend of the age was toward Oriental religions which offered a monotheistic tendency, a practical purpose in offering remission of sin and moral cleansing, and the promise of a happy life beyond.

The Jewish witness among the pagans had remarkable success. The Jewish historian Josephus boasted: "Many of the heathen have come over to our law, some have remained, others unable to tolerate its strictness have fallen off." Then he continues: "Among the masses there has long been a great deal of our worship; there is no Greek or barbarian city nor any nation in which our custom of keeping the Sabbath, fasting, lighting of lamps, and regulations in regard to food, are not observed." And it was Seneca who commented concerning the Jewish race, "Though conquered, have given their laws to the conquerors."

Those influenced by Judaism ranged from the proselyte who renounced paganism and became a full-fledged Jew to the different grades of "God-fearers" who attended the services of instruction and worship in the synagogue but had not actually become full members. Angus points out that there was only one class of regular proselytes, those who broke entirely with their heathen past, accepted circumcision and a "purificatory bath," and made an offering in the Temple. Such proselytes were regarded as new members of the Jewish community and were expected to keep the whole law (Gal. 5:3). These converts were usually more zealous than the Jews by race, and were quite few in number.

Many of the heathen were willing to experiment with various religions, and when Judaism was tried, it retained those who were in earnest. These converts to Judaism found in the synagogue a fellowship of kindred spirits and were strengthened by prayer, by the services of the synagogue, and by stimulating sermons urging men to live a moral life, promising a better era under a Messiah, and holding out the hope of immortality.

IV. The Bible of the Dispersion

In the early years of the Dispersion, the Pentateuch and the remaining books of the Old Testament that had been produced up to that time were written in the Hebrew language. It was such a scroll or a number of such scrolls that Ezra and his assistants used as "they read . . . from the law of God, clearly; and gave the sense, so that the people understood the reading" (Neh. 8:8).

However, as time went by the Aramaic dialect superseded the Hebrew. One illustration of this is that a portion of the book of Daniel was written in the Aramaic. Another illustration is Jesus' loud cry from the cross in which he used the Aramaic dialect. A third illustration is the inscription over the cross of Jesus in Greek, Latin, and Hebrew (Luke 23:38), the word "Hebrew" being a reference to the native Aramaic.

After the conquests of Alexander the Great, Greek became the language of commerce throughout the civilized world. This was especially true in the large Jewish community in Alexandria,

Egypt, where the Jews no longer understood Hebrew, having adopted the language of their everyday business dealings, namely, the Koine Greek.

And since Judaism was the religion of a book, this posed a serious problem. Judaism's sacred book was the Torah, or what we would refer to as the Pentateuch. But the Torah was written in Hebrew which by the third century B.C. was almost an unknown tongue. Thus, if Judaism was to survive, a new translation was necessary.

A romantic account of the origin of the translation of the Old Testament into the Greek, known later as the Septuagint, has become tradition in the so-called *Letter of Aristeas*. In this letter, Aristeas, a courtier in the service of Ptolemy Philadelphus, purports to be writing to his brother Philocrates concerning a recent trip he was supposed to have made to Jerusalem. Aristeas states that the reason he made the journey to the Holy City was because the chief librarian of Alexandria had told King Philadephus that the library needed a translation of the Jewish laws.

The king agreed to send a deputation to the high priest Eleazer in Jerusalem to ask for men to undertake this important assignment. The high priest gladly consented and with the deputation sent back seventy-two accredited scholars, six from each of the twelve tribes of Israel.

The scholars who were chosen for this work carried with them a copy of the Hebrew Scriptures "embossed in gold on fine skins." At a banquet given the scholars, the king tested them with difficult questions. Being satisfied with their answers, he commissioned them to make the translation. The work of the scholars was done on the island of Pharos. At the close of each day, the men compared what was written and thus produced their text. Finally, after seventy-two days the work was finished. When the translation was completed, it was read to the king who expressed his approval. The new translation was enthusiastically received by the Jews.

Though many biblical scholars look upon the letter of Aristeas as legendary, both Philo and Josephus show their acquaintance with it and Josephus adds that "those who were sent to Alexandria as interpreters gave him (Philadelphus) only the books of the law." The early Christian scholar Jerome states that "all Jewish scholars assert that only the five books of Moses were translated by the seventy." And in the *Wisdom of Jesus ben Sirach,* otherwise known as *Ecclesiasticus,* it is stated that all the prophets and some of the Hagiographa had been translated by 132 B.C. so that by the dawn of the Christian era, probably all the remaining writings of the Old Testament were translated into Greek.

Because of its nature, the legend of Aristeas does not cast too much light on the origin of the Septuagint version of the Old Testament. It may be assumed, however, that the Pentateuch may have been translated early in the third century, and that it was for the use of the Jews whose knowledge of their ancestral tongue had lapsed, rather than for the enrichment of the royal library in Alexandria. The importance of the Septuagint version of the Old Testament can hardly be exaggerated. Without this Greek version of the sacred books of the Jewish canon of Scripture, it is hard to see how Judaism could have survived among the Jews of the Dispersion.

Angus notes three important services were rendered by the Septuagint version. (1) It was a great benefit to the Greek-speaking Jews of the Dispersion to have their Bible in a language understood by the people. The Septuagint did for the religious life of the Dispersion what the King James Version of the Bible did for England and the United States and other English-speaking countries, and what Luther's translation of the Bible did for Germany. It became the Bible of Hellenistic Judaism in Asia and Europe, a unique common bond uniting its many readers. The Septuagint version nourished the democratic spirit of piety in the synagogue and prevented Judaism from becoming wholly dependent on a priesthood. The version was also the necessary counterbalance to the disintegrating forces of Hellenism.

(2) The Septuagint became to the Jew a powerful missionary instrument, and to Hellenistic heathenism a religious authority at a time when Greek thought was turning toward the recognition of the necessity of revelation. The appearance of the Septuagint in the synagogue, which was the meeting place of the East and the West, in the language of the mediating Judaeic-Hellenistic philosophy "could not fail to attract attention." Through this version the crowds of "God-fearing" Gentiles heard in the popular Greek language of the people a message of salvation. "And many heathen making trial of different mysteries and looking for some . . . 'sure word of God' in the oracles or in the Oriental religions, discovered in the Septuagint what claimed to be an authoritative and God-inspired guide."

(3) The Septuagint became the first and, for a considerable time, the only Bible of early Christianity and a powerful ally of the gospel. It was the Bible that was used by the apostle Paul and by Luke and by the early missionaries who carried the gospel to "all the world" (Angus, pp. 159–60).

Through the message of the Septuagint version of the Old Testament as expounded in the many synagogues of the Dispersion, the earnest heathen were brought to "the very threshold of the Kingdom of Christ." From the message of its pages was heralded the most perfect salvation offered to the old world. "Her (Israel's) conception of God, though far short of the Christian, was a worthy and attractive one." The message proclaimed from this book was of a "personal self-revealing God, even a Father, a God of strict justice, yet willing to receive and pardon the penitent. Israel declared that God's righteousness demands moral living on the part of man: religion must go hand in hand with morality" (Angus, p. 161).

In many respects the Judaism of the Dispersion was the forerunner of Christianity. It was the Hellenized Judaism of the Dispersion that put into the hands of the early Christians a holy book with the doctrine of inspiration, "the recepticle of an authoritative revelation." Judaism taught Christians the practice and many forms of prayer. She imparted to the Christian her own steadfastness of character, and her zeal to please God with an upright life. She bequeathed to the church her missionary zeal and enthusiasm, her expectancy of a brighter future, her passion for monotheism. Many of the weapons employed by the Christians against the heathen were appropriated from Judaism. The Jewish canon of Scripture was a suggestion to the Christians to formulate an authoritative canon of Scripture for the church. Moreover, the Jews of the Dispersion served as mediators between the East and the West. The Jews of the Dispersion were Oriental in their religion but were Western in their culture, philosophy, language, and enterprise and through the heritage of the Jews of the Dispersion and Oriental religion conquered the western world.

Such are some of the significant contributions of the race to which the promise was given "in thee shall all the families of the earth be blessed" (Gen. 12:3, KJV). This is the people to which the apostle Paul referred when he said: "They are Israelites, and to them belong the sonship, the glory, the covenants, the giving of the law, the worship, and the promises; to them belong the patriarchs, and of their race, according to the flesh, is the Christ" (Rom. 9:4–5).

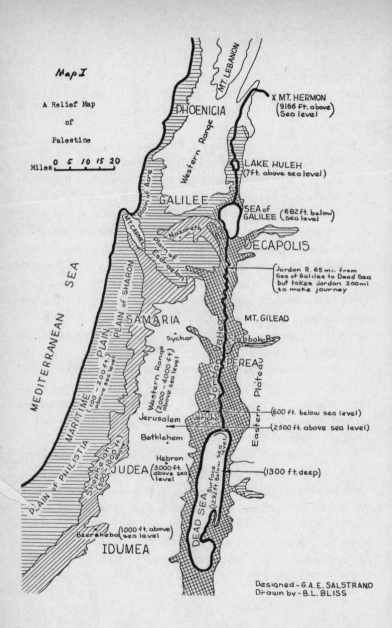

Map I

A Relief Map

of

Palestine

Miles 0 5 10 15 20

MT. LEBANON

PHOENICIA

X MT. HERMON
(9166 Ft. above)
(Sea level)

Western Range

LAKE HULEH
(7 ft. above sea level)

Plain of Acre

GALILEE

SEA of (682 ft. below)
GALILEE (sea level)

MT. CARMEL

Nazareth

DECAPOLIS

Plain of Esdraelon

Jordan R. 65 mi. from
Sea of Galilee to Dead Sea
but takes Jordan 200 mi
to make journey

Plain of Sharon

SAMARIA

MT. GILEAD

Sychar

Jabbok R.

PEREA

MEDITERRANEAN SEA

MARITIME PLAIN (100-200 ft. above sea level)

Western Range
(2,000-4,000 ft.
above sea level)

Jordan Valley

Eastern Plateau

Jerusalem

Jericho

(600 ft. below sea level)

(2500 ft. above sea level)

Bethlehem

Hebron
(3000 ft.
above sea
level)

Shephelah (500-1000 ft.) above

JUDEA

DEAD SEA Surface (1292 ft. below sea level)

(1300 ft. deep)

PLAIN of PHILISTIA

Beersheba (1000 ft. above) sea level

IDUMEA

Designed - G.A.E. SALSTRAND
Drawn by - B.L. BLISS

5. A Unique Land Prepared
Brief History and Geography of Palestine

Palestine has been referred to as "the providential theatre of Divine revelation." It was after he visited this land that Joseph Ernest Renan, the famous author of *The Life of Jesus,* found it to reflect the life and lessons of our Lord "so that it appeared to him a fifth gospel."

In order to come to a better appreciation of the life of our Lord, it is necessary to know something of the historical and geographical backgrounds of his ministry. It was Andre Parrot, the world famous archaeologist, who asked, "How can we know the Word, unless we see it in its proper chronological, historical, and geographical setting?"

Geography has been spoken of as the hook on which the events of history are hung. Again, geography has been called "the eye of history." The background of the history of an event, or a series of events, is the geographical setting which made the history what it was. These observations find their fullest significance when applied to the Bible lands in general and to the land of Palestine in particular.

Usually one of the most important outcomes of a visit to the Bible lands is a strengthened faith that our Lord was a historic person and that the Christian faith is rooted in a very definite historic and geographic context. The Christian who visits the land made sacred by the life and ministry of Jesus, comes away with the realization that "the teaching of Jesus in Galilee and Judea, respectively, has a flavor of the soil." Along this same line of thinking, George Adam Smith said: "A vision of the land itself and its relation to the world, puts the whole Bible into perspective and atmosphere, and enables us to enjoy for the first time, a clear prospect of God's full purpose."

I. Some Interesting Facts Concerning the Land

In the Bible's first reference to the land, it does not refer to it by name, but rather makes it the subject of a promise as God commands Abraham saying, "Get thee out of thy country . . . unto a land that I will show thee" (Gen. 12:1, KJV). Then after his arrival in the land, God again said to him, "Lift up now thine eyes, and look from the place where thou art northward, and southward, and eastward, and westward: for all the land which thou seest, to thee will I give it" (Gen 13:14–15, KJV). Because of these Divine commitments to Abraham and his descendants, this land has become known as "the land of promise" (Heb. 11:9).

The name "Palestine," which is found only once in the Bible (Joel 3:4, KJV), and which became the most popular designation of the land, is derived from one of Israel's arch enemies, the Philistines. It was the Greek historian Herodotus, known as the "father of history," who first used the name Palestine in the fifth century B.C.

Through the centuries, Palestine has gone by many names. In Ruth 1:1 it was called the *land*. In Zechariah 2:12 it is the *holy land*. In Hosea 9:3 it is the *Lord's land*. In Daniel 11:16 it is the *glorious land*, and in 1 Samuel 13:19 it is the *land of Israel*. It was also called *Canaan* because the first inhabitants were the descendants of Canaan, the grandson of Noah (Gen. 9:18).

As one looks at a globe of the world, Palestine is only a tiny spot, "a narrow streak." In one day it would be possible to drive a modern car around the borders of the old kingdom of Israel. The traditional north and south terminals of Dan and Beersheba are only 150 miles apart. At its northern end the land is only thirty miles wide, while the width of the southern end is some seventy miles. Historic Palestine included some 10,000 square miles of territory and was slightly larger than the state of Vermont. In comparison the state of Israel before its conquests of 1967 included some 8,000 square miles.

In no country of the world can such variety of landscape, climate, and produce be found as in the land of Palestine. This is due to extremes in height and depth of altitude, to moisture-laden coast breezes, to winds from the desert, and to the fact that this land lies at the point where the temperate zone meets the semitropical. Within a period of only six months time, it is possible to experience arctic cold in the vicinity of Mount Hermon and intense heat in the plain of Jordan, near the Dead Sea. Some six miles east of Jerusalem it never snows, while on Mount Hermon there are patches where the snow never melts.

II. The Physical Divisions of the Land

In our Lord's day Palestine was Roman Judea. Its principle regions were: (1) *Galilee,* the northern province where Jesus grew to manhood and carried on an extensive ministry; (2) *Samaria,* the rugged central highland which became the Kingdom of Israel after Solomon's United Kingdom was divided; and (3) *Judah* (also known as Judea), the southern region ending at the border of Idumea. This land consisted of a varied terrain which, running from north to south, may be divided into five long strips or zones.

1. The Maritime Plain

Beginning at the Mediterranean seacoast the first division is the Maritime Plain. Broken only by Mount Carmel, which juts out to within only a few yards from the sea, the Maritime Plain extends from the River Leontes in the north to the desert beyond Gaza in the south. From north to south this plain is in turn divided into the Plain of Acre (north of Mount Carmel), the Plain of Sharon, and the Plain of Philistia. This is a very fertile sandy plain which varies in altitude from one- to two-hundred feet above sea level and has an average width of about twelve miles.

2. The Shephelah

Moving eastward, the next geographic division is the Shephelah or Piedmont territory. It includes the foothill country of Samaria and Judea, extending from Mount Carmel on the north to Beersheba in the south. Ranging from five hundred to a thousand feet in altitude, this foothill country formed a natural barrier between the Maritime Plain and the mountains.

3. The Western Range

The third geographic division of Palestine is the Western Range of mountains. Beginning in Galilee this range of mountains extends southward into the Negev and varies in altitude from one hundred to four thousand feet. Near the southern end of the Western Range is located the city of Jerusalem some 2,500 feet above sea level.

4. The Jordan Valley System

The fourth geographic division of Palestine is the Jordan Valley System. At the northern extremity stands Mount Hermon reaching a height of 9,166 feet, the high point in Palestine. The Jordan River originates in the foothills of Mount Hermon and the Lebanon

Mountains as a small mountain stream, and flows first through the small lake of Huleh, seven feet above sea level, thence south through the Sea of Galilee which is 682 feet below sea level. Shaped somewhat like a pear, the Sea of Galilee is thirteen miles long and seven miles wide with the narrower portion of the lake to the south.

Leaving the Sea of Galilee, the River Jordan flows south to the Dead Sea. Though this is a distance of only seventy miles the winding river requires two hundred miles to make the descent. The Dead Sea, the surface of which is 1,292 feet below sea level, is also 1,300 feet deep, which makes it the lowest spot on the earth's surface. The Dead Sea is forty-six miles long and ten miles wide and has no outlet, except by evaporation. Twenty-five percent of its solution is minerals, or five times the amount usually carried in ocean water. It is called "dead" because no marine life is found in its waters and its shores are barren of vegetation and animal life.

5. The Eastern Plateau

East of the Jordan Valley is the Eastern Plateau. From north to south, this territory was divided into Basham, Gilead, Moab, and Edom. In the days of Jesus' ministry the northern territory was known as the tetrarchy of Herod Philip. To the south was the Decapolis, a territory which received its name from the ten Greek cities which it included. In Jesus' day the southern division of the Eastern Plateau was the Roman province Perea. Herod Antipas who was the ruler of Galilee also governed Perea.

6. The Plain of Esdraelon

Unlike the other divisions of Palestine, the Plain of Esdraelon runs from the Mediterranean Sea on the west, cutting across the Western Range. The plain is a rough triangle with one point at Mount Carmel, the second point terminating in the hills of Samaria, and the third at Mount Tabor. This triangular plain which is about 200 to 300 feet above the level of the Mediterranean Sea is a very fertile area which is drained by the Kishon River. Since the valleys of this plain connect with all the divisions of the land, this plain is often referred to as the key of Palestine. This plain came into prominence in the ministries of Elijah and Elisha. Through this plain passed the great international highway of which the Latin name was the Via Maris, meaning "the way of the sea" (Isa. 9:1). One branch of this famous road crossed the Jordan north of the Sea of Galilee and passed through Capernaum. The other branch crossed the Jordan below the Sea of Galilee after which they came together and continued through the Plain of Esdraelon to the city of Accho, the present Acre. The main section of the plain is often called the Valley of Megiddo, which through the ages has been one of the great battlefields of the nations.

III. Some Special Features of the Land

1. The Capital City

Known as Salem in the days of Abraham (Gen. 14:18; Ps. 76:2) and captured from the Jebusites by the armies led by King David, Jerusalem came to be known as the City of David and was also called Zion. In beautiful poetry the psalmist sang about his beloved city saying: "Great is the Lord and greatly to be praised in the city of our God, in the mountain of his holiness. Beautiful for situation, the joy of the whole earth, is Mount Zion, on the sides of the north, the city of the great King. God is known in her palaces for a refuge" (Ps. 48:1-3, KJV).

God was speaking of this city when he said through the prophet Ezekiel: "This is Jerusalem; I have set her in the midst of the nations, and countries are round about her" (5:5, ASV). In the book of Ezekiel, Jerusalem is said to be "in the middle of the earth" (38:12, ASV), which is no doubt a reference to her central geographical position in relation to the earth.

The noted scholar Carl Ritter has been referred to as "the father of modern geography." Discussing the city of Jerusalem in the fourth volume of his *Comparative Geography of Palestine and the Sinaitic Peninsula,* Ritter wrote of the strategic position and of the influence of the Holy City saying:

> Jerusalem—built in the heart of Judea, away from all great lines of communication which cross the East; separated and protected from the powers lying eastward from it by the Dead Sea, from those at the north and west by almost inaccessible footpaths, and by the Mediterranean Sea, and from those at the south by the broad wastes of desert which stretch away to Egypt; situated on the rocky foundation, destitute of rich flora, almost without fields, without a river, almost void of springs and any productive soil—has nevertheless gained a place among the great cities of the globe, which, among those of Europe, can only be compared to Rome and Constantinople. And in many respects it has reached a place higher than they, and affected the world more powerfully; for Jerusalem, as the city of David, as *par eminence* the Temple City, has not only had the advantages of age, riches, splendor, trade, luxury, art, and conquest, like the great European capitals; but in the diffusion of its central idea of the unity of God who must be worshiped in spirit and in truth, in opposition to the idolatries of the rest of the world, it has before, and more eminently since, the birth of Christ carried to the ends of the earth a light which, though having to contend with doubt, falsehood, and superstition, has been enabled to cleave through them all, to dissipate the clouds, and to warm and quicken the mind of man through the whole Western World; to affect already that of the East, and to afford assurances that it will do more and more" (pp. 1–2).

In a similar vein of thought, George Adam Smith, the celebrated

Bible scholar, wrote this tribute to the city of Jerusalem:

> So lofty an influence was exercised by Jerusalem some centuries before
> the appearance of Jesus Christ; yet it was only prophetic of the worship
> she drew from the whole world as the scene of His passion, His cross
> and His grave. Though other great cities of Christendom, Antioch,
> Alexandria, Carthage, and Rome, were by far her superiors in philoso-
> phy and spiritual empire, Jerusalem remains the religious center of the
> earth—whose frame was even conceived as poised upon her rocks—the
> home of the faith, the goal of most distant pilgrimages, and the original
> of the heavenly city, which would one day descend from God among
> men. In all, it had been thirty-three centuries of history climbing slowly
> to its central fact of all time, and then toppling down upon itself in
> a ruin that has almost obliterated the scenes and monuments of the
> life which set her alone among the cities of the world.

2. The Secluded Province of Judea

From the Jordan River to the Philistine Plain, the Province of
Judea was only thirty miles wide and from Geba in the north to
Beersheba in the south is fifty-five miles. The total size of the
province of Judea included only 1,500 square miles. Thus Judea
was only slightly larger than the state of Rhode Island.

The territory occupied by the province of Judea was a barren,
rugged, and rocky land. It was a land of mountains and wilderness
of which the southern part was especially wild and desolate. In
addition, Judea was very dry. In the entire province there were only
seven streams which flowed the whole year.

The mountainous character of Judea contributed to the sturdi-
ness of her people. Most of them were shepherds. For centuries
the inhabitants had little contact with the outside world, being
hemmed in by rocky walls. For a long time these people took no
part in the wars of their neighbors, and they held aloof from
progress and conquest. It was this very isolation which helped

Judea to hold out against the great world powers, Babylon, Egypt, and Rome. Judea's existence continued a whole century and a half after the Northern Kingdom was conquered.

3. The Strategic Position of Palestine

Located at the juncture of three continents—Africa, Asia, and Europe—the position of Palestine made it a bridgehead coveted by the world conquerors. Through Palestine, especially along the Maritime Plain and the Plain of Esdraelon, ran the trade routes of the ancient world. The land was a halfway stop between the great river basins of the Tigris, Euphrates, and the Nile. It was the battleground of the empires that rose and fell in the rich Nile Valley to the west and the fertile Tigris-Euphrates Valley to the east. On this route the customs and the trade of Asia, Greece, and Africa mingled. In two directions the people of Palestine faced the desert and the nomads of the desert. On the other sides they faced the men of all the then known world who were making history.

Thus, the people of Palestine were in touch with all the nations, and yet by a paradox of history by their mountain homes and natural barriers, they were isolated from the outside world. The currents of world commerce flowed along the edge of Palestine and yet this land was sufficiently separated to develop its own life. The people of this land enjoyed a certain amount of solitude, but at the same time there was the possibility of fruitful contact with the outside world. In their struggle for existence the people of the land developed a sense of dependency upon God "together with an overwhelming perception of the sublime and universal."

4. The Providential Provisions

God's providential preparation of the unique land of Palestine helped to set the stage for the life and ministry of our Lord and the proclamation of the Christian faith. J. McKee Adams says in his splendid study entitled *Biblical Backgrounds:*

> The selection of Canaan, thus situated in the geographical center of the ancient world, was clearly related to a higher purpose; that out of its manifold contacts should come a spiritual contribution to color and determine the whole course of world history. The all-seeing eye that chose the narrow strip of territory bordering on the Mediterranean looked beyond the horizon to adjacent countries and to islands of the sea. Regarded in this manner, Canaan had no limitation; it was prophetic of a master plan which included the world in its scope and interests. Central in its religious life, where all oriental cults met and blended, except one; central in its political contacts, where all kingdoms struggled for supremacy; central in its social complexion, where the best and worst were thrown together into a great melting pot of cultural amalgamation; central in its economic and commercial dependence, the object of materialistic invasions by neighboring peoples, it was also central in a larger plan which brought together all interests to serve a higher and more far-reaching purpose. We hold that its central position was designed because of the *Central Mission* associated with Israel (pp. 85–86).

6. The Messianic Hope
A Swelling Stream of Messianic Expectancy

An important phase of the preparation of the civilized world for the advent of the Savior and the Christian faith was the messianic hope of Judaism. This expectation was an important element of the Jewish faith. It was a part of the very warp and woof of the content of the record of the Old Testament.

The teachings of Hebrew Scripture concerning a Coming One made the Jews a people who looked to the future. When conditions around them were discouraging, they were sustained by this hope. They lived for the day the promised Messiah would be established on the throne of His Kingdom.

I. The Hope Introduced

The title "Messiah" is derived from the Hebrew word *mashiach,* which means to anoint. As used by the Jews this word means "Anointed One." In one sense, it was used of anyone who held his office by "Divine right" or "by the grace of God." The prophet Isaiah applied this title to the Persian monarch Cyrus (45:1). It meant that this ruler was appointed or raised up to fulfil God's purpose by his policy of allowing the Jews to return to their homeland to rebuild their Temple and the defenses of Jerusalem. In this sense Cyrus was the anointed of the Lord, even though he did not realize that this was true or accept the Lord as his God.

In ancient Israel two outstanding offices were "messianic," namely, the priesthood and the kingship. This was true in the sense that men were consecrated to serve in these offices by the solemn ceremony of anointing. For this reason the king was spoken of as "The Lord's anointed" and the chief priest was known as "the anointed."

The king and the priest were both accorded the Hebrew title *mashiach,* meaning messiah. It is the Hebrew word *mashiach,* which in the Septuagint Greek version of the Old Testament is rendered *christos,* and which in English is transliterated "Christ." The king and the priest in differing ways both served as mediators between God and their people. This was also true of the prophet, although he was not usually installed in his office by anointing. (An exception is 1 Kings 19:16b.) But even though oil was not used in setting them apart, the prophets were referred to as God's anointed men (1 Chron. 16:22).

The title "messiah," however, was primarily given to the kings of the dynasty of David. It came into use in the latter part of the Old Testament history and was used to designate the descendant of David who would restore the vanishing glories of the era when the great king reigned over all the tribes of Israel.

In his *Discourses on Prophecy* Patrick Fairbairn likens the messianic emphasis of the Old Testament to a swelling stream saying: "It appears somewhat like a river, small in its beginnings, and though proceeding, yet often losing itself for ages underground, then bursting forth anew with increased violence, and at last rising into a swollen stream—greatest by far when it has come within prospect of termination" (pp. 335–36, quoted from Jasper A. Huffman, *The Messianic Hope in Both Testaments).*

An interesting characteristic of messianic prophecy is that it builds on truth already revealed. R. H. Payne in his Bampton Lectures entitled *Prophecy a Preparation for Christ* brings out this truth as follows:

> Men never do understand anything unless already in their minds they have some kindred ideas, something that leads up to the new thought which they are required to master. Our knowledge grows, but it is by the gradual accumulation of thought upon thought upon thought, and by following out ideas already gained to their legitimate conclusions. God followed this rule even in the supernatural knowledge bestowed upon the prophets. It was a growing light, a gradual dawning, and no flash of lightning, illuminating everything for one moment with ghastly splendor, to be succeeded immediately by a deeper more oppressive gloom. . . . Carefully and with prayer, the prophets studied the teachings of their predecessors, and by use of the light already given were made fit for more light, and to be spokesmen of Jehovah in teaching ever more clearly . . . those truths which have regenerated mankind (quoted from Milton S. Terry, *Biblical Hermeneutics,* p. 442).

In this chapter we will trace the development of the messianic idea from the first germ of promise in Eden to the occasion when the aged Simeon in the Temple in Jerusalem took the infant Jesus in his arms and sang his song of praise. The main passages of the Old Testament dealing with messianic truth will be studied and the thoughts of biblical scholars, ancient and modern, will be focused on these verses.

II. Some Leading Messianic Promises

The messianic hope began with a promise. It was the fall in Eden that necessitated a Savior by whom the race might be restored to God. Our first parents had sinned. In the moment of their failure God announced his gracious promise to redeem the race.

1. Seed of the Woman.—The first faint note of messianic promise is recorded in Genesis 3:15 which reads:

> I will put enmity between you and the woman,
>   and between your seed and her seed;
> he shall bruise your head,
>   and you shall bruise his heel.

This passage is called by Old Testament scholars the *Protevangelium*. It contains messianic prophecy in germ. Our first parents, who had so recently transgressed God's command, did not understand the full meaning of the promise given to them. But the message of God kindled hope in their hearts. It painted a picture of life on the background of death. This new hope caused Adam to name his wife Eve. The name Eve means *life,* or *life giver.* Adam gave his wife this name because she was to be the mother of all living.

2. Descendant of Shem.—Another faint messianic promise is found in Genesis 9:26–27. This message indicates that the Coming One is to be from the Semitic race. Shem was given preeminence in religion, a blessing he was to share with his brothers.

3. Seed of Abraham.—It was Abraham, the son of Terah and a descendant of Shem, to whom God gave a peculiar promise relating to the messianic hope. In Genesis 12:2–3 (KJV) the promise reads: "I will bless thee and make thy name great; and thou shalt be a blessing: . . . and in thee shall all families of the earth be blessed."

Abraham was to be a blessing to all the families of the earth. This promise referred to in Genesis 18:18 is repeated in 22:18 where it is connected with an innumerable posterity (cf. 26:4 and 32:13). In the New Testament these passages were given a messianic interpretation by Peter (Acts 3:25) and by Paul (Gal. 3:8).

4. Ruler from the Tribe of Judah.—The twelve stalwart sons of Jacob were gathered around him as the aged patriarch neared death. In such solemn circumstances the aged patriarch designated his son Judah to be the ancestor of the coming Deliverer. The prophetic announcement of Genesis 49:10 states:

> The scepter shall not depart from Judah,
>   nor the ruler's staff from between his feet,
> until he comes to whom it belongs;
>   and to him shall be the obedience of the peoples.

5. A Mighty Conqueror.—The next messianic passage is Numbers 24:17 which reads:

> I see him, but not now;
>   I behold him, but not nigh:
> a star shall come forth out of Jacob,
>   and a scepter shall rise out of Israel;
> it shall crush the forehead of Moab,
>   and break down all the sons of Sheth.

The man who uttered this prophecy was Balaam of Aram in Mesopotamia, a man of weak character who knew the true God. Balak the king of the Moabites had employed Balaam to curse Israel. But when Balaam tried to curse Israel he found it impossible. Finally, he yielded to God's Spirit and uttered these words.

While the New Testament writers do not claim the words of Balaam as a prophecy fulfilled in Christ, they do apply to our Lord other Old Testament passages which speak of a mighty conqueror. Two such passages are Psalms 2 and 110.

The Balaam passage, however, was used by the early Christians as one of the sections which bore testimony to Jesus. Justin Martyr in his *Dialogue with Trypho the Jew* says: "And that he (Jesus) should rise like a star from the seed of Abraham, Moses showed beforehand when he said: 'A star shall rise out of Jacob and a leader from Israel'. "

6. *The Prophet.*—Another messianic passage is found in Deuteronomy 18:15 as follows: "The Lord your God will raise up for you a prophet like me from among you, from your brethren— him you shall heed."

The prophet like Moses is referred to several times in the New Testament. John the Baptist knew about this prophet. When he was asked, "Are you that prophet?" he answered, "No" (John 1:21).

When Jesus fed the multitude, the reaction of the people was: "This is indeed the prophet who is to come into the world!"(John 6:14). The food Jesus had provided reminded them of the manna Jehovah had given in the wilderness. They thought Jesus was the new prophet, the second Moses.

On the mount of transfiguration the three disciples saw the vision of Jesus in glory along with Moses and Elijah and they heard a heavenly voice saying: "This is my beloved Son; listen to him" (Mark 9:7). The words "listen to him" echo the final words of Moses' prophecy, namely; "him you shall heed." They indicate that Jesus was the prophet of whom Moses had spoken.

During the Feast of Tabernacles Jesus stood in the Temple court and called saying: "If any one thirst, let him come to me and drink" (John 7:37). Because Jesus' invitation reminded the people of how Moses obtained water from the rock they said, "This is really the prophet" (v. 40).

Two more times in the book of Acts Jesus was identified with the prophet like Moses. In the court of the Temple in Jerusalem Peter actually quoted the words of Deuteronomy 18:15, referring to Jesus (3:22). Again, when Stephen was on trial before the Sanhedrin he quoted the words of Moses about the coming prophet (7:37).

7. *Offspring of King David.*—For forty years David had reigned as the king of Israel. The first capital was Hebron, but the capital city during his last seven years was the mountain fortress Jerusalem, which had been captured from the Jebusites.

During the years of David's reign in Jerusalem, many new buildings had been erected to house the various branches of the government of Israel. But the good king was troubled by the fact that the house of God was old and in a state of disrepair. The wilderness tabernacle was not adequate for the new age.

The king brooded over the need for a new house of worship and determined to lead Israel in building a new sanctuary. One day he shared his dream with God's prophet Nathan, who at first thought this would be a good idea. The Lord, however, sent Nathan back to David with the message, "You may not build a house for my name, for you are a warrior and have shed blood" (1 Chron. 28:3).

At first the spirit of King David was crushed. Such was the background of the Lord's reassurance through the prophet that he would build him a house. The promise which follows indicates that what the Lord was speaking of was a dynasty, a dynasty that would be eternal. Then the prophet spoke to David the words found in 2 Samuel 7:12-17, commonly known as the Davidic Covenant.

In the first part of the Davidic Covenant the Lord said, "When your days are fulfilled . . . I will raise up your son after you, . . . and I will establish his kingdom" (v. 13). This was a reference to David's son Solomon who succeeded to the throne of Israel. He was destined to build God's house, which became known as Solomon's Temple.

Then the Lord announced, "I will establish the throne of his kingdom forever" (v. 13). This passage refers to David's descendant, Christ. It was quoted to Mary by the Angel Gabriel when he announced that she would give birth to Jesus (Luke 1:32–33). David was to be the head of a dynasty that would endure for ever in Jesus Christ (cf. v. 16).

8. *A Royal Priest.*—Because every verse in Psalm 110 applies to Christ, it has been referred to as the most distinctive of the messianic psalms. This psalm not only sets forth Messiah's kingship, but that he would be a priest king. "You are a priest for ever after the order of Melchizedek" (v. 4).

This is the passage the writer of the epistle to the Hebrews used to find authority for the priestly side of Jesus' messianic work (Heb. 5:6,10). Commenting on this use of Psalm 110:4, F. F. Bruce in his *Second Thoughts on the Dead Sea Scrolls* says: "There is sound historical justification for ascribing a priesthood of this order to the Davidic Messiah, for it is extremely probable that after David's capture of Jerusalem he and his successors viewed themselves as heirs to the ancient royal priesthood exercised by Melchizedek and other pre-Israelite rulers of the city.

"The writer of Hebrews does not dwell on the historical basis for his argument: . . . but by developing the doctrine of Jesus' perpetual priesthood in terms of the Old Testament portrayal of Melchizedek he has given the church its classic exposition of this phase of our Lord's Messianic dignity and service" (p. 89).

III. The Messianic Hope in the Psalms

The Hebrew word for Psalms is *Tehillim* which means "praises." This book was given the name "Psalms" in the Greek Septuagint Version of the Old Testament. It was the hymnbook or psalter regularly used in the Temple worship.

In this section attention will be given to the messianic psalms or the psalms applied to Christ in the New Testament. Some of

these are messianic in a typical way, which means that they depict
the experiences of the writer, but are applied to Christ. Other
psalms are predictive. Of these Psalms 2, 45, and 110 predict the
messianic king. In Psalm 45:6 Messiah is God. In Psalm 110 he
is the priest-king and David's Lord. In Psalm 2 he is God's Son
to be worshiped. Psalm 22 speaks of his suffering. His sacrifice is
spoken of in Psalm 40. In Psalm 16:10–11 the resurrection of the
Messiah is predicted. In Psalm 89 the Messiah is the one who
brings to completion the Davidic Covenant. It is this solemn covenant Jehovah made with King David (2 Sam. 7:4–17) which is the
germ of the messianic psalms (Ps. 89:34–36).

Some of the outstanding experiences of our Lord were foreshadowed in type or predicted in prophetic word in the Psalms. Jesus
said that the things spoken of him in the Psalms would be fulfilled
(Luke 24:44).

1. The Coming and Sacrifice of Messiah.—The sacrifice of Christ
is foretold in Psalm 40:6–10. Of this passage verses 6–8 are quoted
in Hebrews 10:5–7 which reads:

> Sacrifices and offerings thou hast not desired,
> but a body hast thou prepared for me;
> in burnt offerings and sin offerings
>   thou hast taken no pleasure.
> Then I said, "Lo, I have come to do thy will, O God,"
> as it is written of me in the roll of the book.

In the verses which follow this passage in Hebrews the writer
indicates that the statement, "Lo, I have come" signifies the end
of Levitical sacrifices by the coming of Christ and offering of his
own body once for all.

2. The Betrayal.—The betrayal of Christ is foreshadowed in
Psalm 41:9–11. It speaks of treachery, and Judas was the traitor

who betrayed Christ. This passage is referred to in Acts 1:16 in connection with the story of how a successor to Judas was chosen. This passage was given messianic significance when our Lord quoted it referring to the treachery of Judas (John 13:18).

3. *The Crucifixion.*—Psalm 22 has been called the crucifixion psalm. Five times this psalm is quoted in the New Testament and referred to Christ. The first twenty-one verses vividly portray in prophecy what happened to Jesus when he died on the cross.

The psalm opens with the heartrending words, "My God, my God, why hast thou forsaken me?" The next statement reveals the utter loneliness of the sufferer as he asks, "Why art thou so far from helping me?" As Jesus hung on the cross, he quoted the first statement and thus applied it to himself (Matt. 27:45–46).

The psalmist speaks of the spectators who mocked (vv. 7–8). The Synoptic Gospels paint the pathetic picture of the fulfilment of these words as Jesus hung on the cross and was mocked by the passing crowds (Matt. 27:39–46).

The dreadful thirst (v. 15), the piercing of the hands and the feet (v. 16), the parting of the garments and the casting of lots for the robe (v. 18) were all foretold. These and many other indignities were experienced by Jesus during the crucifixion (John 9:23–24).

It is believed that these words were written by the psalmist David, who, as the prophet of God, foresaw the sufferings of Christ and the glory to follow.

The crucifixion is also foreshadowed in Psalm 69 in which the psalmist tells of "those who hate me without cause" (v. 4). This was true of Jesus. What happened when Jesus died on the cross is depicted in verses 20–21 (cf. Matt. 27:34,48).

4. *The Resurrection.*—The resurrection of Christ is predicted in Psalm 16:8–11. On the day of Pentecost Peter quoted these words

and referred them to Jesus (Acts 2:24–32). Paul in his sermon in the synagogue in Antioch of Pisidia (Acts 13:14–42) cited Psalm 16:10. He said that this passage did not refer to King David who died and whose body "saw corruption," but Jesus "whom God raised up saw no corruption" (Acts 13:35–37).

5. *The Ascension.*—Psalm 68:18 is referred to in Ephesians 4:8 where Paul interprets this verse and applies it to Christ. The one who ascended, said Paul, is the one who descended, meaning, from heaven to earth. This one was Christ who triumphed gloriously and gave the church the gifts of the ministry. The psalm is not directly messianic, but in his use of this psalm Paul is applying the general picture of the triumph of God to the work of Christ.

6. *The Royal Psalms.*—God's covenant with King David promising him an eternal dynasty is reaffirmed in Psalm 89:34–36. This covenant promising King David that there would always be someone to sit on his throne is again cited in Psalm 132:11 where the psalmist said:

> The Lord swore to David a sure oath
>   from which he will not turn back:
> "One of the sons of your body
>   I will set on your throne."

In Psalm 118:19–25 Messiah is the rejected stone which became the head of the corner. In connection with Jesus' rejection by the Jews this passage is quoted six times in the New Testament (cf. Matt. 21:42; Acts 4:11 and 1 Pet. 2:4–10).

Psalm 2 has been called Messiah's "coronation hymn." It tells of one who is called "the Lord's anointed" against whom the kings of the earth rebel. The Lord, however, establishes his throne and

invites all to kiss him in submission. The messianic nature of the
first two verses of this psalm is indicated in Acts 4:23–28.

While Psalm 72 is not applied to Christ in the New Testament
it gives a fitting picture of the kingship and the kingdom of the
Messiah. It speaks of the reign of the King. His reign shall be
widespread, righteous, prosperous, and happy. While most of what
is written in this psalm could be applied to Solomon, there are some
statements that cannot be applied to Solomon but must be applied
to Christ.

Psalm 110 has been spoken of as "the most distinctive of the
messianic psalms because "every passage applies to Christ."

IV. The Messianic Hope in the Prophets

Because he gives the fullest and clearest exposition of the gospel
of Christ to be found in the Old Testament Isaiah is known as the
"evangelical prophet." His book is especially rich in the many
passages it contains which refer to the Messiah. It is Isaiah who
foretells that Messiah is to be born of a virgin (7:14, KJV). In 9:6–7
the prophet foretells the birth of a great ruler who would be a
descendant of King David. This ruler is to bring peace to the
nations (2:4). He will be a descendant of Jesse (the father of David)
(11:1), "him shall the nations seek" (v. 10). The Coming One will
be "a light to the nations" (42:6; 49:6).

Four passages in Isaiah designate the Coming One as the Servant
of Jehovah, namely, 42:1–9; 49:1–13; 50:4–11; 52:13 to 53:12.
Chapter 53 describes the Messiah as *the suffering servant.* "He was
despised and rejected" (v. 3). "He was oppressed, and he was
afflicted; . . . like a lamb [he was] led to the slaughter" (v. 7), and
"he makes himself an offering for sin" (v. 10). This servant "poured
out his soul to death" and "bore the sin of many" (v. 12).

In Isaiah 61:1–3 the Messiah says: "The Spirit of the Lord is upon me, because the Lord has anointed me to bring good tidings to the afflicted," etc. At the beginning of his ministry Jesus read this passage in his home synagogue and applied these words to himself saying, "Today this scripture has been fulfilled in your hearing" (Luke 4:21).

The brief prophecy of Micah makes a significant contribution to the messianic hope. It designates the birthplace of the deliverer. "But thou, Bethlehem, Ephratah, though thou be little among the thousands of Judah, yet out of thee shall he come forth unto me that is to be ruler in Israel: whose goings forth have been from old, from everlasting" (5:2, KJV). It was this passage that made it possible for the chief priests and the scribes to answer Herod's question as to where Christ would be born (Matt. 2:6).

Jeremiah contains three important messianic passages: (1) The first is a description of the coming Messiah (23:5-6). He will be David's son, "a righteous Branch" (v. 5). He will "reign as king and deal wisely." He will "execute justice and righteousness in the land" (v. 5). He will be called by the messianic title, "The Lord our righteousness" (v. 6). (2) The second states that Messiah will introduce a new covenant (31:31-34; cf. Heb. 8:10-12; 10:16; Rom. 11:27). Instead of being written on tables of stone, this covenant will be written on the hearts of the people of God (v. 33). No new Decalogue will be introduced, but power will be given to obey the old. (3) The third passage (33:14-26) repeats several ideas previously stated in the first. It then goes on to reaffirm the Davidic Covenant (2 Sam. 7:16; 1 Kings 2:4) saying: "David shall never lack a man to sit on the throne of the house of Israel" (v. 17). He goes on to say, "The Levitical priests shall never lack a man . . . to make sacrifices for ever" (v. 18; cf. Psalm 110:4; Heb. 5:6; 6:20; 7:17,21).

There are several prophecies in Zechariah which refer to the

Coming One. Using a messianic title "the Branch," Zechariah goes on to tell of the coming priest-king (6:12–13). He delivered the prophecy that Messiah would enter Jerusalem on an ass (9:9) which Jesus fulfilled (Matt. 21:4–5). The prophecy of the sale for thirty pieces of silver was delivered by Zechariah (11:12–13), and Matthew stated that this prophecy was fulfilled when Judas sold Jesus for thirty pieces of silver (27:9–10). The piercing of the side of Jesus may also be alluded to by this prophet (12:10).

The statesman-prophet Daniel from the midst of two world empires of his day saw the four empires of history, and beyond them the fifth universal empire. Near the close of his vision he saw a stone "cut out by no human hand" which struck the image representing Gentile rule. In his vision Daniel saw the image struck on the feet and ground it to powder, and in its stead arose the Divine Kingdom set up by the God of heaven "which shall never be destroyed." While each of the four kingdoms grew mighty and perished, the fifth kingdom will endure (Dan. 2:44). Daniel in the prophecy of the seventy weeks (9:24) announced the time of Messiah's first advent. It is the only statement in the Old Testament giving the time Messiah was to come and be "cut off."

Malachi was the last of the prophets. In his prophecy we find a strange mixture of the material and the spiritual aspects of the messianic hope. The way will be prepared for the Messiah who will be "as a refiner and purifer of silver, and he will purify the sons of Levi and refine them like gold and silver." He also referred to Messiah as "the sun of righteousness . . . with healing in its wings" (4:2–3).

V. Messianic Expectancy from Malachi to Christ

Malachi was the last of the prophets of the Old Testament. The final historical books were Ezra, Nehemiah, and Esther. Of these personalities Nehemiah and Malachi were contemporaries. From the close of the period in which these men labored to the advent of the Savior was a little more than four hundred years. During this time no inspired historian or prophet appeared. This time span is known as the interbiblical period or the four silent centuries.

During this interbiblical period the national idealism of Judaism was theocratic. The Jews believed Jehovah should be the direct ruler of the land he had given them. When they returned from the captivity, they cherished this hope. They looked upon themselves as God's chosen race, the special objects of his care and favor. But the history of the Jews gave evidence that the high ideals concerning this relationship had never been realized. As a result they turned their eyes more and more to the future.

1. Highlights of Messianic Expectancy in Later Judaism

Concerning this messianic expectancy H. E. Dana in *The New Testament World* says: "Again in later Judaism there appears . . . the idea of a personal Messiah as a divinely appointed leader who shall become the national champion against Israel's foes" (p. 131). Then Dana continues saying, "On one essential point interbiblical Judaism agrees. God would eventually deliver his people from heathen bondage and elevate them to the supreme place of power and influence among the nations."

During this period it was thought that God would bring in the Golden Age for Israel in the person of a great prophet who would fulfil the messianic role. This aspect of the messianic hope was quite generally sustained and perpetuated by a yearning in the hearts of the more devout for a return of the spirit of prophecy. This expectation was voiced by the woman of Samaria who said to Jesus, "I know that Messiah is coming; . . . when he comes, he will show us all things" (John 4:25).

Also during this period the idea of Messiah being a king and a priest became a widely accepted view among the Jews (cf. Ps. 110:4). Some think that one reason this view became widely accepted was that from the time of Simon Maccabaeus the kingly and priestly offices were combined in the Hasmonean rulers of Judah. Simon was the first to occupy this dual office. (See chapter 3.)

Many in Judaism looked for a supernatural Messiah. As the earthly powers oppressed them, many Jews became increasingly dissatisfied with the world order of their day. Their view of the Messiah became more and more transcendent. They despaired of human deliverance, even under Divine appointment and leadership. Intervention must come from heaven. Messiah was conceived of as an angelic being who would be sent from heaven by Jehovah to deliver his people.

In this period, however, the most popular view was that of a descendant of King David. He would be a warrior king who would be a political champion and a military hero to rally to his standard the Jews from every nation and lead them to victory against their enemies.

2. Messianic Expectancy in the Qumran Community

In 1947 a Bedouin shepherd boy followed a stray goat and discovered a cave northwest of the Dead Sea. In the cave he found broken jars of pottery which held scrolls inscribed in ancient Hebrew. These scrolls and others found in the same area are now known as the Dead Sea Scrolls, the greatest manuscript discovery of modern times.

A number of scholars carefully unrolled the crumbling scrolls and translated their messages. It is now believed that what was discovered was the library of an ascetic sect, possibly Essenes, now known as the Qumran community.

Among the discovered scrolls are copies of almost all the books of the Old Testament. Other scrolls, written in Hebrew, Aramaic, and Greek, gave details of the sect's religious beliefs and practices.

In 1956 F. F. Bruce wrote *Second Thoughts on the Dead Sea Scrolls.* In a chapter on "The Messianic Hope" Bruce compares the hope of the Qumran community with the messianic hope of the early church. Based on his research Bruce learned some very interesting things about the beliefs of the Qumran community concerning their messianic hope. A fragment of one manuscript found in Cave 4 was a compilation of *Patriarchal Blessings* with Jacob's blessing on his son Judah expanded as follows:

A Ruler shall not depart from the tribe of Judah. The explanation reads: "When dominion comes for Israel (there shall never) fail an enthroned one therein for David. For the 'ruler's staff' is the covenant of kingship, and the 'feet' are families of Israel."

Until he comes. The explanation again reads: "Who is the rightful Messiah, the shoot of David, for to him and to his descendants has been given the covenant of kingship over his people for everlasting generations" (p. 80).

Commenting on these passages as explained by Qumran community Bruce says: "What is of chief importance is that Jacob's blessing of Judah is a prediction of the coming Davidic Messiah. The enigmatic 'Shiloh' is paraphrased" (p. 81).

Another document from Cave 4 is an anthology of passages referring to the glorious prospects awaiting the house of David. In the following extract from it the prophet Nathan's promises to David about the perpetuity of his dynasty are coupled with a prophecy at the end of the book of Amos about the future restoration of the Davidic dynasty.

Expounding 2 Samuel 7:11–14, the Qumran writer states: "This is the shoot of David, who is to arise with the Expounder of the Law . . . in Zion in the latter days, as it is written:

And I will raise up the booth of David that is fallen (Amos 9:11). The explanation reads, "That is David's fallen booth, but he will arise hereafter to deliver Israel" (p. 81). Bruce then states: "This is evidence of the Qumran community's expectation of the anointed prince of the house of David.

Another interesting quotation is from Numbers 24:15–17 where the Mesopotamian prophet Balaam foresees the rise of a military conqueror in Israel (probably King David). This is followed by the blessing pronounced by Moses upon the priestly tribe of Levi in Deuteronomy 33:8–11. Commenting upon these statements Bruce says: "The way in which these quotations are brought together suggests that the writer looked for the advent of a great prophet, a great captain or prince, and a great priest" (p. 82).

Later Bruce says: "One of the names the community described itself was the community of Israel and Aaron (*i.e.,* laymen and priests). And it probably expected both the Messiah of Israel and the Messiah of Aaron to emerge from its ranks." Further on Bruce continues: "Even the prophets could be described collectively as God's anointed, because they acted under His commission, even though no oil had been poured on their heads" (p. 83).

Bruce then summarizes and draws a comparison: "In any case we have found an interesting point of contact between Qumran and Christianity—a point of contact and also a point of cleavage. The Qumran community and the early Christians agreed that in the days of fulfilment of all that the Old Testament prophets had said there would arise a great prophet, a great captain and ruler, and a great priest. But these three figures remained distinct in Qumran expectation, whereas the early Christians saw them unified in the person of Christ" (pp. 83–84).

Balaam's prophecy about a star out of Jacob was a favorite with the Qumran community. The Qumran documents show that the community was looking for a valiant hero who would lead the faithful to victory in war against the sons of darkness. Qumran also expected an anointed priest, who, in the new age, would lead the state, and would receive orders from the Davidic Messiah.

Finally summarizing his chapter on "The Messianic Hope" Bruce says: "The Qumran community, then, had its messianic doctrine. One point in which it differs from the messianic doctrine of the New Testament, as we have said, is its expectation of three personages at the end of the age, whereas the Christian Messiah is Prophet and Priest and King all in one" (p. 89).

3. Summary of Messianic Expectancy in Later Judaism

In his chapter on "Preparation for Christianity" in Volume I of *A Manual of Church History,* Albert Henry Newman deals with "Messianic Expectations" (pp. 63–64). The following is a summary of Newman's findings:

Nothing is more characteristic of later Judaism than the prominence and definiteness of its messianic expectations.

While the glorious future of the nation was not lost sight of by the later Jews, far more stress was laid by them on the relation of the individual and of the non-Jewish world to the messianic kingdom.

The doctrines of immortality and resurrection come more clearly into the consciousness of the people. Eschatological elements naturally occupy a more prominent place in their messianic expectations.

God is now definitely thought of as the King of the world, and Messiah as judging and ruling the world on God's behalf. The Messiah is ready to appear as soon as the people should repent and

perfectly fulfil the law. A single day of repentance on the part of
the nation would usher in Messiah's kingdom.

In some accounts his secret presence is assumed, and his revelation is delayed by the sins of the people. His appearing is conceived
of as sudden and accompanied by miraculous displays of power.
The appearing of Messiah was to be followed by a marshalling of
the heathen powers for a final conflict and the overthrow of these
hosts of evil by the power of God.

The renovation and purification of Jerusalem follows. The new
city is to surpass the splendor of the old.

The dispersed are next to be gathered and are to participate in
a glorious and joyful kingdom which, centering in Jerusalem and
Palestine, is to extend throughout the world. War and strife shall
cease, and righteousness and benevolence and virtue shall prevail.
Suffering and disease shall be no more. Men will live as much as
a thousand years. Childbirth will be painless and physical effort
without weariness. Some thought of the earthly kingdom as everlasting, others looked upon it as a prelude to a still more glorious
heavenly kingdom.

The next stage in the panorama is the universal resurrection.
This is to be followed by final judgment. Jewish eschatology provided for an intermediate state between death and resurrection in
which the righteous souls are happy and the wicked suffer.

From the views already set forth it is evident that the idea of
a suffering and sin-atoning Messiah had little place in the Jewish
thought of the age under consideration. If such passages as Isaiah
53 were messianically interpreted at all, little emphasis was placed
upon the character and purpose of the Messiah there set forth.

Concluding Remarks

This brings to a close of our study of messianic expectancy in the Old Testament and in later Judaism. The Coming One was to be of "the seed of the woman," of Semitic stock, a descendent of Abraham, and from the tribe of Judah. He was to be a mighty deliverer, a great prophet "like Moses," a priest "after the order of Melchisedec," and a king who would be a descendant of David. He would be a suffering Messiah whose reign would be universal.

Announcing the coming birth of Jesus the angel Gabriel said to Mary:

> He will be great, and will be called the Son of the Most High;
> and the Lord God will give to him the throne of his father David,
> and he will reign over the house of Jacob for ever;
> and of his kingdom there will be no end (Luke 2:32–33).

To the woman of Samaria Jesus identified himself as the expected Messiah (John 4:25–26). At the height of his Galilean ministry the people sought to take Jesus by force and make him king (John 6:15). After the Galilean ministry as Jesus was giving special training to the twelve he was delighted when Peter, speaking for the disciples, confessed him as the Messiah saying, "You are the Christ, the Son of the living God" (Matt. 16:16).

It was as Israel's king that Jesus made his royal entry into Jerusalem. And when he was crucified the inscription of the charge against him read, "The King of the Jews."

Following his resurrection, while walking to Emmaus with two disciples, Jesus taught that he was the fulfilment of the many messianic promises of the Old Testament. Reporting what happened on that journey, Luke says: "And beginning with Moses and all the prophets, he interpreted to them in all the scriptures the things concerning himself" (24:27).

Later the same day as Jesus met with a group of his disciples
he told them, "Everything written about me in the law of Moses
and the prophets and the psalms must be fulfilled" (Luke 24:44).

Once again, this time in the book of Acts, Luke gives his readers
another glimpse of the messianic expectancy that prevailed in the
days of Jesus' ministry. It was when Jesus was meeting with his
disciples for the last time before his ascension that they asked him,
"Lord, will you at this time restore the kingdom to Israel?" (1:6).

One of the many saints of later Judaism living in Jerusalem at
the time of Jesus' birth was an aged man named Simeon. Luke says
that Simeon was "righteous and devout, looking for the consola-
tion of Israel." In fact, this man had been assured "by the Holy
Spirit" that he would not die until he had seen the Messiah, "the
Lord's Christ" (2:25–26).

Prompted by the Spirit, this old man entered the Temple at the
same time Joseph and Mary came to dedicate Jesus, their firstborn
son. And when the aged Simeon saw the child Jesus, he immediately "took him up in his arms and blessed God" saying:

> Lord, now lettest thou thy servant depart in peace,
>   according to thy word;
> for mine eyes have seen thy salvation
> which thou hast prepared in the presence of all peoples,
> a light for revelation to the Gentiles,
> and for glory to thy people Israel (Luke 2:27–32).

7. The Civilized World Prepared Part I

Oriental and Greek Influences

The civilized world of the first century surrounded the Mediterranean Sea and extended from Africa to Gaul, now known as France. This area contained the highest civilization of that age, and one of the highest of any age. In this expanding dominion of Rome the peoples of many subject races lived and shared their heritages, and made their contributions of influence.

In the New Testament world the two cultures which were the most visible were those of Greece and of Rome. For this reason the civilization of the first century is called Graeco-Roman. In addition to the more visible Graeco-Roman elements of the culture of that period, there was substratum of influence not so clearly visible which was Oriental and Jewish.

I. The Oriental and Jewish Influences

Any careful student of New Testament history soon becomes aware of the Oriental element which underlies the civilized world of the first century. The many mystery religions in the background of the New Testament were largely Oriental. The Jewish people, whose pre-Christian history was traced in the preceding chapters, were Oriental in race and thought. In its early beginnings the character of Christianity was Oriental. Even to this present day the basic beliefs of our faith are of Oriental origin. Many other influences of Oriental thought can be discerned in the culture of that day, especially in the Mediterranean area.

When Christianity made its first appeal to the Gentile world, it found "a religious psychology susceptible to its message." The appeal of the early Christian leaders was effective because of these influences which had permeated the first-century world. Oriental religions were widely accepted. This was especially true in the great population centers such as Alexandria, Athens, and Rome.

The Oriental contributions to Christianity came mostly through Judaism. While the extent and the effects of these contributions cannot be definitely determined, the fact of this heritage is beyond question.

Speaking of these contributions and their implications H. E. Dana in *The New Testament World* says: "This, however, should in no way prove a disturbing factor to our evangelical faith. If God was pleased to use contacts of Oriental thought in order to bring into clearer view some elements of his revelation, the original authority is none the less divine because such instrumentalities were used. We must accept the means God has used, rather than assuming the prerogative of dictating the means he should have used" (p. 19).

In the early ages of history, Hebrew theology was quite similar to that of the Babylonians and Persians. Together they held similar ideas on "the immortality of the soul, the existence of the spirit world, the eternal rewards of human conduct, and the resurrection of the dead."

The Hebrews had been in touch with the Babylonians and Persians from ancient times of antiquity. This contact became intimate during the captivity and the years that followed. Many of the names of Jews who lived in that period are of Babylonian and

Persian origin. The Jewish writers reveal more distinct concepts in eschatology after their contact with the Persians. Further developments in their angelology can also be discerned after the restoration. The Persian word meaning "paradise" which had reference to the abode of the righteous dead came into frequent use among the Jews during the Persian period. Following the Persian period the demonology of Judaism was developed.

It is likely that the responses of Judaism to the Babylonian and Persian sources were unconscious reactions. When the restoration came, it was the faithful remnant of Jews who returned from the Mesopotamian valley to reestablish their homeland and worship in Judah. The results of the Babylonian and Persian contacts were mainly in new modes of thought and expression.

Commenting on the influences of these contributions of Oriental thought to the New Testament, Dana says that "this Oriental substratum . . . brought out certain elements of thought in bold relief by the conflict which it offered. The positive contributions came through Judaism; the negative contributions came through Hellenistic philosophy and Grecian Oriental religions" (p. 20).

Judaism embraces the life, thought, and literary products of the Jews. It had its chief center in Jerusalem and its primary operation in Palestine. Judaism has certain distinctives which set it apart from the Oriental world and require that it be treated as a distinct phase of ancient life. From Judaism Christianity received its greatest heritage.

Jesus was a Jew and it was he who said, "Salvation is from the Jews" (John 4:22). Paul, who in his day was the greatest propagator of the Christian faith, was also a Jew. The "doctrines, practice, psychology and experience in first-century Christianity were predominantly Jewish, though advancing constantly in the Hellenistic direction" (p. 21).

Judaism made a tremendous contribution to the preparation of the world for Christianity. It was a preparation for the gospel of Christ, both directly and indirectly. The God of the Old Testament is the God of the New. He is "holy, just, merciful, self-revealing, and loving." The great doctrines of the Old Testament such as creation, the fall of man, holiness, and the coming Messiah were assimilated into Christianity and in it were more fully developed. The Jewish synagogues in the Hellenistic centers of the Roman Empire provided openings for the early preaching of the gospel. Many of the first converts to Christianity were won in the synagogues. These converts were both Jews and Gentiles. The Gentiles who became Christians were already proselytes to the Jewish faith who had abandoned paganism in search of a purer and more satisfying faith.

II. Grecian Influences

A well-known proverb states: "The entire first-century world went to school to Hellas." In a wider sense this has also been true through the centuries, among the nations of the civilized world, since the blossoming of the Greek civilization known as Hellenism.

In the centuries preceding the birth of Christ a unique people inhabited the land of Hellas, which later became known as Greece. The culture produced by the early Greeks is called Hellenism was "the greatest intellectual influence which has ever been exercised over the thought life of mankind" (p. 178).

Concerning this Greek culture H. E. Dana says: "The Jewish worship has without doubt been the supreme benefit [to mankind], but it failed to prove effective until it was universalized and rationalized by Greek culture. When the old wine-skin of Jewish legalism proved insufficient, the new wine-skin of Greek thought offered a ready recepticale for the gospel of Christ."

Without the vital force of this Greek culture, it would be difficult to conceive of Christianity achieving the tremendous progress it made in the first three centuries. Moreover, as one contemplates the unique historical situation at the beginning of the Christian Era "it appears that Greek culture was waiting to become the servant of the new religion" (pp. 178–179).

1. Greek Backgrounds

The culture of the Greeks had its roots in the Orient. Their culture was a heritage of the Cretan civilization, which many centuries before was assimilated by the Achean Greeks of the Mycenean age. Albert J. Trever says: "History reveals no real break between the civilization of Greece and the Orient, but a constant interpretation" (*The History of Ancient Civilization,* Vol. I, p. 149).

The ancient Greeks called themselves Hellenes and their land Hellas. Their original home was the Hellenic peninsula which is now occupied by modern Greece. It is a territory of less than 30,000 square miles, or about the size of the state of Maine. Northern and western Greece, however, played a very small part in Hellenic history. It was the people of the southern and eastern part of ancient Greece who through colonization turned the whole Mediterranean basin into a Greek world. And it was when some of the early Hellenes established a colony in southern Italy that the Romans first called them Greeks.

The Hellenic peninsula is predominantly a land of mountains. Most of this area is made up of bare rocky soil supporting only scrub trees and scant vegetation. Less than one third of the land is under cultivation. For this reason a Greek historian wrote: "To Hellas poverty was always a foster-sister." It was because of the scarcity of the natural resources of their land that many Greeks colonized in the Mediterranean area, or turned to commerce.

This racial heritage of the Greeks was "a happy mixture of northern European and Mediterranean elements." This union of racial strains "endowed them with the ability to create a unique and brilliant civilization far beyond anything that had preceded them."

2. Greek Education

During the centuries preceding the advent of the Savior, Greek scholarship made remarkable achievements. One of the greatest exponents of science was Aristotle. He emphasized the inductive method of reasoning, which is basic to science. The geographical theories of Strabo are valued sources of historical information. Some of the pedagogical methods of Quintilian are still used in modern education. The mathematicians of Alexandria made important astronomical calculations which vary little from the results of modern astronomy. Machinery and mechanical engineering had reached a high state of development. Remarkable advances were made in surgery and medicine.

In the Graeco-Roman world teaching was a popular and honorable profession. Academic achievement was given recognition through distinctive titles such as, philosopher, doctor, or sophist. The education of the day was preeminently Greek. The universities in which the Romans sought higher education were all Greek. Greek universities were located in Athens, Rhodes, Tarsus, Antioch, Alexandria, and Marseilles. Alexandria with its university, its library, and its museum was an outstanding center of learning. (See chapter 4.)

3. Greek Language

The Greek language has been referred to as the most perfect vehicle of human thought ever devised. Concerning this language

Trever in his *History of Ancient Civilization,* Volume I says: "The masterful Greek language, . . . with its concise directness in saying exactly without ambiguity what it means, its compactness and flexibility, its ability to express the finest shades of thought and feeling—even the tone of voice, gesture or play of features—its picturesque abundance of metaphor and figure, its balance of clauses, and its musical quality, is a notable example of the creative imagination and other great qualities of the Hellenic mind" (p. 151).

It is of interest to trace the process by which the Greek language became the vernacular of the world of the first century. In the fifth century B.C. the Attic dialect used by the Athenians came into wide use with the growth of the Athenian empire. Though the empire was destroyed by the end of the fifth century, the dialect of Athens, namely, that of classical literature, became the language of Alexander and the soldiers and merchants of the Hellenistic world from 338 to 146 B.C. It was this language which became modified and enriched and which was spread throughout the Mediterranean world. The dialect of the common man grew out of this process. It was into this language that the Jews of Alexandria translated the Old Testament, and it was this language known as the Koine Greek that the early Christians used.

When Christianity began its westward progress, the Koine dialect of the Greek language was waiting as the ready instrument of communication which the early Christian missionaries used. Moreover, this language was a very effective means of communication. It was "the most richly and accurately expressive language which human history has known. Its possibilities of subtle distinction in the expression thought are vast, and the writers of the New Testament were remarkably adept at using the finer capacities of this language." Having made this evaluation, Dana in *The New Testa-*

ment World says: "It is no exaggeration that the Greek New Testament is the most richly expressive text in all literature" (p. 180).

4. Major Greek Philosophy

In its origin philosophy arises from the faculty of the human mind called wonder. Man looks upon his environment and begins to ponder and question. Thus, consciousness through the senses perceives its environment, and reason seeks answers. This effort to attempt to form an intelligent interpretation of environment is philosophy.

By nature Christianity is susceptible to the influence of philosophy. This is because philosophy arose as a product of reflection. In its infancy Christianity consisted of an interpretation of Christ and his relation to the believer's experience. For this reason the message of the early apostles made its first appeal to the intellect. It provoked thought. It called for reflection. It challenged comparison with the results of thought which had already been achieved. This brought the Christian message into immediate contact with the current philosophies of the Graeco-Roman world.

The dawn of Greek philosophy came about 600 B.C. and reached its zenith in the philosophies of two of the greatest thinkers of all time, Plato and Aristotle. Dana divides the development of philosophy into three phases: physical, ethical and theological. S. Angus in his *Environment of Early Christianity* concurs with this division and observes that this is "the natural order of man's progress, taking first the outward look, then the inner look, and the upward: of nature, man, God" (p. 174).

a. The Physical Phase

The pioneer of Greek philosophy was Thales of Miletus who lived about 600 B.C. He thought he found the ultimate substance in water. Anaximander, a follower of Thales, thought he found the ultimate substance in fire. Anaximenes, another follower of Thales, thought he found the essential substance in air. Anaxagoras (500–428 B.C.) proposed the hypothesis that "mind was the permanent and controlling principle of the natural order."

To Heraclitus (536–475 B.C.) the basis of reality was fire. He was deeply impressed by the fact of perpetual change. He saw fire as the most radical and thorough agent of change. He said: "All things are exchanged for fire, and fire for all things, as wares are exchanged for gold, and gold for wares." For Heraclitus fire was the essence of permanence and law the principle of permanence.

The most important forward movement of the naturalistic group of philosophers was represented by Anaxagoras (500–428 B.C.). He proposed that mind was the permanent and controlling principle of the natural order.

b. The Ethical Phase

A whole chapter in the history of ethical philosophy belongs to the Sophists. They were aggressive individualists in thought and life. They emphasized "the dignity of man and freedom in religious political and intellectual life." The principle of Protagoras that "man is the measure of all things" stimulated a reexamination of all the old foundations of human life. "Traditional institutions and beliefs were brought under the white light of criticism. Nothing was too sacred to escape." The logical result was a negative skepticism in speculative philosophy (Trever, p. 348).

One of the most important products of the Sophist philosophy was Socrates (470–399 B.C.). In his philosophical system Socrates appropriated the best of Sophism and differed widely from the views of the typical Sophists of his day. Like the Sophists Socrates built his philosophy on the idea that whatever is right is right in its own nature. He believed in the validity of the conscience and the reality of final truth and justice, and he urged men to live in accordance with their inner sense of right. He also inaugurated a search for the supreme expression of Good.

But by his fearless criticism of all institutions and beliefs Socrates incurred the wrath of the citizens of Athens, who charged that he was "a corrupter of youth" and one who "did not believe in the gods in whom the city believes." After having drained the cup of the deadly hemlock, Socrates spent the moments while the poison was doing its work, discussing with his companions the problem of immortality. "His death placed the seal of martyrdom upon his noble life, and greatly increased his influence."

Socrates gave a strong impetus to the development of ethical monotheism, and thus became a source of moral and religious philosophy from which western Christianity has made appropriations. Moreover, it was Socrates who inspired Plato, "whose germinal thought has had more influence in the history of Western culture than that of any man save his pupil Aristotle."

c. The Theological Phase

In introducing his discussion of Hellenic philosophy in the fourth century B.C., Trever says: "Amid the social and political decay of the city-state, when the Hellenic passion for self-determination was fast commiting suicide, Greek philosophy rose to its height of vitality and creativeness in Plato and Aristotle (p. 435).

Plato (427–346 B.C.) lived through "the terrible years of the Peloponnesian War, the fall of Athens, the oligarchic revolutions, and the hopeless interstate strife of the fourth century B.C." His entire life was affected by these experiences. The execution of his friend and revered teacher, Socrates, alienated him from the democracy. To find a solution for the problems of his age he turned to philosophy. About 378 B.C. he founded his school in Athens.

In his theory of knowledge Plato went beyond his teacher. The Socratic concepts of universal truths, established by induction, Plato declared to be the only true objective realities. He regarded objects of sense as only imperfect shadows of these realities. He taught that "the real world is spiritual, abiding, and unseen, and is apprehended by pure reason." This point of view is in philosophy known as Idealism. To the general concept he gave the Pythagorean term "Idea." Plato's ideas, however, are objective realities, and objects of sense are real only to the degree that they embody the perfect idea. He believed that the highest idea is the Idea of Good or God, the supreme reason, the ultimate cause and purpose of all, the World Soul, whose earthly analogy is the Sun in the heavens.

In ethics, Plato taught the Socratic principle that virtue is knowledge or right thinking, which is wisdom, and that this kind of knowledge is possible and can be taught. His emphasis on virtue was even more central, and had its root in his doctrine of ideas. He said, "The supreme good is not happiness, but likeness to God."

Aristotle was Plato's most brilliant pupil. After the death of his father Aristotle left his home and journeyed to Athens where he studied under Plato and assisted in his academy until Plato died. Later he spent some years in Macedon tutoring the young prince Alexander. About 335 he opened his own school in Athens.

Socrates has often been referred to as the first scholar and the first bookish man. He marked the transition of Hellenic culture from thought and discovery to scholarly criticism, and an encyclopaedic systemizing of past knowledge.

Theories must conform to observed facts, insisted Socrates. In his Metaphysics he sought to clarify the relation between ideas and things. While making the idea the final reality, Plato left the relation between the idea and the final reality vague. In Aristotle's practical mind, on the other hand, neither could exist separately, and reality was a combination of both. Universal truths, though of supreme value, can best be arrived at through a study of particulars. Trever says he also taught that "Above all natural substances is the absolute transcendent God, pure spirit, the 'prime mover' though himself unmovable, eternal, good, 'thought eternally thinking itself' " (p. 441).

5. Other Philosophies

The *Cynics* taught that the supreme good lies in pure and rational judgments and the suppression of all human desires. In his teaching they followed Socrates, who regarded happiness and virtue as in some way clearly related.

According to the *Cyrenaics* pleasure is the supreme good, and hence the supreme concern of life is to secure from each passing moment the maximum enjoyment, subordinating all else to this aim.

Stoicism is an advanced and more refined development of Cynicism. Zeno (342–270 B.C.) was not a Greek but a Hellenized Semite from Cyprus. Stoicism was a mixture of philosophical ideas from Plato, Oriental religions, the old polytheisms, Chaldean astrology and magic. Stoicism gets its name from the Greek word *stoa* which means porch or portico. This philosophy is named after the stoa or portico in Athens where Zeno taught.

According to Stoic ethics virtue is the only pure good. The "wise man" alone is truly wealthy, happy, and free, since he alone knows how to use wealth wisely, and live independent of externals. This individualistic code of ethics also has a social side expressed in the statement "through human reason all are united to Divine Reason, all are brothers" (Trever, p. 516).

The Stoic view of nature was materialistic. The Stoic god, though rational and good, is impersonal, and his system is fatalistic in that nothing can happen in nature or life other than what does happen. No real evil can eventually triumph nor any good be finally defeated. The present world will finally end in a great conflagration.

Later Stoicism developed into a religion which became a substitute for the dead civic religion, both to the upper classes and to the masses. Stoic ethics found a religious sanction in the relation of the human to the Divine Reason, and the ". . . wise man gained inner peace through faith in this relationship."

Epicureanism is a descendant of the teachings of the Cyrenaics and Sophists. The founder was Epicurus (341–270 B.C.), who began teaching in his own garden.

Epicurus rejected law and urged pleasure as the chief good. He outlines this position saying: "When we say that pleasure is the end we do not mean the pleasure of the libertine and the pleasures of mere enjoyment . . . It is not drinking and revellings . . . nor tables loaded with dainties . . . but sober reasoning to discover what must be sought and avoided, and why, and to banish fancies that have most power over men's souls."

We need, however, to distinguish between theoretical Epicureanism and practical Epicureanism. There is vast difference between the speculative views of the high-minded philosopher and the actual conduct of his self-indulgent follower. As accepted and applied by most of its adherents, Epicureanism was employed as a philosophical excuse for the grossest forms of sensuality. In the first century it was regarded as a synonym for moral corruption.

Other philosophies can be called *eclectic.* This word means a

combination of views. About the second century B.C. there began
to be a blending of philosophies from both Greek and Oriental
sources which produced an eclectic form of philosophy known as
gnosticism. It resulted from selecting and combining current
schools of thought, and it presented a confusing variety of views.

An important form of eclectic philosophy in the background of
the New Testament is found in the teachings of Philo, the great
Alexandrian Jew who has been referred to as "the greatest mind
Hellenistic Judaism produced." Though Philo was Jew he was also
an enthusiastic admirer of the philosophic thought of Hellenism.
In Philo we meet a man thoroughly trained in Greek philosophy
but at the same time a fervent Jew. He sought to set forth the
teachings of Moses and the traditions of Israel in terms of Greek
philosophy and the Jewish religion. The basis of his philosophy was
religion. "He was an intense mystic, and endowed with a marvel-
ous degree of spiritual discernment. Often his religious conceptions
approached remarkably near Christian ideas" (Dana, p. 197).

One of Philo's most intimate contacts with Christian teaching
was his view of mediation. This he expressed in the Greek term
Logos which means "word" (cf., John 1:1, 14). He held the Jewish
concept of the transcendence of God, and yet his mystical nature
and his ideas called for contact between man and God. To reconcile
this conflict he devised the mediatorial function of the Logos.

Philo's heart hungered for fellowship with God, whom he believed it impossible for his sinful soul to reach, so he seized upon
the idea of the *Logos,* which was already a well-known concept in
the religio-philosophical mind of his day, and found it a satisfac-
tory means of assuring himself of peace and fellowship with God
(Dana, p. 198). Recognizing the influence of the eclectic philosophy of Philo in the background of the writings of the New Testament will lead to a better understanding of the Gospel of John and

the later New Testament epistles.

The confusion and uncertainty of these various systems of philosophy convinced many that there could be no final and dependable knowledge. For this reason many turned to Skepticism, the philosophy of probability, which had as its slogan: "What is truth?"

Such were the varying and conflicting currents of thought into which flowed the mighty stream of Christianity with its message of redemption.

8. The Civilized World Prepared Part II
The Political and Religious Situation

The three greatest historical movements of the past centuries converged in the birth of Jesus Christ. The best known and the most beautiful of all birth narratives reports the way God brought together these three currents of history when "the time was right."

Jesus was born of a young Jewish maiden as predicted in the prophecies of the Jewish Scriptures. His birth, his life, and his ministry were recorded in the universal language of Greece. And it was the government of Rome which required Joseph and Mary to visit Bethlehem "in the fulness of time."

Thus, even before the sages of the distant Orient brought their gifts to the newborn king, Jew, Greek, and Roman stood unseen around the Bethlehem manger, gathered by the silent urge of an irresistible providence. Each from his own history brought valuable gifts to prepare the world for the ministry of the Savior. The Jew brought the wealth of his religious heritage. The Greek brought his near perfect language and his keenly trained mind. Imperial Rome presented an organized world.

Having already considered the contributions of Judaism and Hellenism to the world into which Jesus was born, the purpose of this final chapter is to survey the political situation and the varied religious scene which prevailed in the Mediterranean world of the first century. Of course, we have room for only a brief summary.

I. Politically the World Was Roman

S. Angus called the founding of the Roman Empire as "the greatest political achievement ever accomplished." He also stated that "Christianity came in the heyday of 'the grandeur that was Rome'." Hegel in his *Philosophy of Religion* said: "The Roman world forms the supremely important point of transition to the Christian religion, the indispensable middle term."

Referring to Julius Caesar as the founder of the Roman Empire, Angus described him as "the most wonderful man that Rome or any other country produced." Referring to Octavian, Angus said, "a great man was on hand for the occasion who realized that supreme power was the only possible solution." The Empire had its formal beginning January 16, 27 B.C. when Octavian received the title Augustus. Under republican forms he ruled as emperor, controlling legislative administration and the armies.

1. Roman Peace

One of the great benefits conferred by the Roman Empire to the civilized world was the Roman peace which was designated *Pax Romana* and which continued for some two hundred years. There had been no peace among the nations since the days of Alexander the Great. The quarrels of the rulers who succeeded Alexander and the aggressions of the Roman republic had kept the nations in constant turmoil. Universal peace was first realized with the beginning of the reign of Augustus in 27 B.C. In all the countries around the Mediterranean Sea and from Britain to the Euphrates the world had rest. Rome made an end of her own civil wars and stopped the wars among nations. Rome ruled her territory well, and the Empire united Greeks, Romans, and Jews, all under one government. Thus, Rome blended the nations and prepared them for Christianity. For the first time the world could be spoken of as a universal humanity, an economy with "humanity living under a uniform system of government."

2. Cosmopolitanism

The Roman Empire made a substantial contribution to the cosmopolitanism which had set in as a result of the conquests and Hellenizing activities of Alexander the Great and his successors. Under the Roman Empire all of the national barriers were removed and the great cities such as Rome, Alexandria, Antioch, and Athens became the meeting places of all races and languages. Soldiers from all parts of the world became companions. Thousands of Greek slaves of fine education and culture contributed much to this cosmopolitanism. These slaves in many cases were far superior to their masters in culture and became their teachers. Then, too, as pointed out in a previous chapter, the Jews of the Dispersion were scattered into every part of the empire.

Angus in *The Environment of Early Christianity,* commenting on this cosmopolitanism observed: "Christ came at the one time in history when all civilized nations lived, as it were, under one roof, when the happiness of mankind depended on the will of one, when all were able to communicate in one language, when men were unanimous as to the perils and needs of the world, when there was peace on earth, when there was 'one empire, one universal language, a common development toward monotheism, and a common yearning for saviours' " (pp. 222–23).

Related to this cosmopolitanism was a great impetus to a corresponding eclecticism of thought. The intermixture of the races and the mutual exchange of thought was to provide a background for Christianity. Each people discovered how much it had in common with its neighbors. For some time Stoicism had been preaching the doctrine of civic and ethical brotherhood of humanity. In the fusion of the philosophic systems emphasis shifted from the city-state with its extreme political nationalism, to the moral and human point of view. Thus, all humanity was "reduced to equality before the One." One of the Greek poets expressed this feeling by saying, "We are his offspring."

3. Roman Jurisprudence

The political unity of the Roman Empire was maintained by the application of Roman law to the citizens in all parts of the Empire. The importance of this law was daily pressed upon the Romans and subjects of the Empire by the impartial Roman courts. This Roman law grew out of the customary law of the early monarchy. During the early republic in the fifth century before Christ, this law was codified in Twelve Tables, an essential part of the curriculum used in the education of every Roman boy. The realization that the great principles of Roman law were also shared by other nations in their laws grew upon the Romans. Because of their position in administering justice, the Romans made it their business to become acquainted with the national legal systems of the foreigners now a part of the Empire. Thus, the Twelve Tables of Roman law were enriched by the laws of other nations. This uniform system of good laws taught men to obey and respect authority, and it proved a leveling and civilizing power in the empire. As one writer put it, "The universal law of Rome was the pedagogue of the universal law of the gospel."

4. Travel

At the time of the birth of Christ there was a great deal of travel. Pompey had cleared the Mediterranean Sea of pirates which made the sea an important means of communication. Large and small ships sailed the sea in countless numbers. The importance of the Mediterranean as a means of communication during this period is amply illustrated by Paul's many records of sea voyages.

Rome also built a great system of roads which radiated from the golden milestone in the Roman forum of the Eternal City in every direction. These great roads bound the civilized world together. Built for the rapid movement of the military from place to place, with the dawn of the *Pax Romana,* all these roads became alive with "a galaxy of caravans and traders." Commerce revived and was carried on under more favorable conditions than any that existed until the past century. A careful study of the life of Paul reveals that he made good use of these great arteries of trade.

5. Tolerance

The freedom the Roman authorities granted to the religions of all nations greatly favored the growth of the infant Christianity. Since Judaism was a legal religion and since Christianity was at first thought of by the Romans as a sect of Judaism, Christian missionaries were usually protected by the government. The attitude of the Roman government toward religion is illustrated by the case of the Jews dragging Paul before the new proconsul Gallio in Corinth and Gallio's dismissal of the case (Acts 18:12–16).

II. Religiously the Picture Was Varied

1. The Greek Religion

The religion of ancient Greece has been aptly described as an anthropomorphic polytheism. To the Greeks their gods were but superior human beings with the cravings and weaknesses of human nature. Their gods transcended the plane of common humanity in power but not in character. The religious concepts of the Greeks found their most elaborate literary expression in the Homeric poems. In fact, the writings of Homer have on occasion been referred to as the Bible of the Greeks. The Greek religion like the Roman was national. The Athenian state considered that it was its duty to promote and safeguard the religion of the commonwealth. The Greek gods were more personal and realistic than the gods of Rome. But the worship of the Greeks was only a sort of hero worship. The gods were national rather than universal.

That the worship of many local gods could lead to the confusion of the worshipers can be seen in the following quotation from Dana: "Since the pagan deities of the former age had been local, belonging to a single nation, city, or household, when people began to move from place to place, they confronted a serious religious difficulty. If one left his native locality, he thereby severed his connection with the national or family gods. It was difficult to become accustomed to the peculiarities and worship of the new god or gods in the locality to which he moved. On the other hand, as new neighbors came in from other localities, bringing new gods with them, perhaps with more attractive qualities and inducements, one of a profound religious temperament felt inclined to take in the new gods alongside the old ones. As a result, the common people became confused" (pp. 237–38).

Thus, many of the more cultured Greeks lost faith in the gods their fathers worshiped. As the effects of the Greek culture increased its sway over the first-century mind, the more intelligent leaders began to think and to question and soon realized that the one who was really a god could not consistently be subject to local or racial limitations. Thus, the old national and local religions were threatened with extinction.

2. The Roman Religion

Prior to the dawn of the Christian era, as the result of the influx of Greek culture and philosophy along with new religious influences, the popular interest in the old religion of Rome began to recede. The old national religions and systems of belief proved unable to soothe the urgent moral and spiritual demands of man's nature. This left a spiritual vacuum which the religions of that day could not fill. As a result, moral bankruptcy was imminent. The old Roman religion of abstract virtues had gone into formalism. It proved to be too cold for human hearts. Men could no longer find the field of their moral activity in the religion of the state. There was a crying need for a positive religion, the need for a perfect ideal life as a dynamic to give inspiration to ordinary human beings. Men felt an urgent need for a new revelation and for a fresh vision of the knowledge of God.

3. Religious Unrest

About the time of the founding of the early Roman Empire there began a period of tremendous unrest. Men tried philosophy, magic, astrology, and foreign cults as they sought inner peace. Especially popular were the mystery religions of the Orient which seemed to offer more in spiritual and emotional aid than the religions of Greece and Rome. Depicting briefly the appeal of three of these religions, Earle E. Cairns in *Christianity Through the Centuries* says: "The worship of Cybele the great earth mother, was brought to Rome from Phrygia. The worship of this goddess of fertility had in it rites, such as the drama of the death and resurrection of Cybele's consort, Attis, that which seemed to meet the emotional needs of men. The worship of Isis, imported from Egypt, was similar to that of Cybele with its emphasis upon death and resurrection. Mithraism, an import from Persia, made special appeal to the soldiers of the Roman Empire. It has a December festival, an evil one, a miraculous born saviour—Mithra, a dead and resurrected god and chapels of worship" (p. 43).

All of these religions emphasized the savior-god. The worship of Cybele called for the sacrifice of a bull and the baptism of worshipers in the bull's blood. Mythraism featured sacrificial meals. Because of the widespread influence of these religions the demands of Christianity seemed reasonable.

4. The Jewish Religion

In contrast to the Greeks the Jews did not seek to discover God by the processes of human reason. They assumed the existence of God and granted to him the worship they felt he was due. They were influenced toward this mode of thought by the fact that God sought them and revealed himself to them in history by his appearances to Abraham and to the other leaders of their race. "Jerusalem became the symbol of a positive religious preparation for the coming of Christianity." Salvation was to be "of the Jews."

One of the unique contributions of the Jews to religious thought was monotheism. In striking contrast to the worship of many gods in pagan religions, Judaism gave emphasis to a sound spiritual monotheism. After the return from the Babylonian captivity, the Jews never again lapsed into idolatry. The message of Moses to them was one that demanded allegiance to the one true God of all the earth. To the Jews the gods of the pagans were mere idols which their prophets had condemned. By means of the Dispersion, this monotheism was spread throughout the Mediterranean world during the three centuries preceding the coming of Christ.

In the moral portion of its legal system Judaism offered the world the purest ethical system in existence. The high moral standard of the Ten Commandments was in sharp contrast to the ethical systems which prevailed among the nations at the time of the coming of the Savior. "To the Jews, sin was not external, mechanical, contractural failure of the Greeks and Romans, but it was a violation of the known will of God, a violation which expressed itself in an impure heart and then in overt external acts of sin. The moral and spiritual approach of the Old Testament made for a doctrine of sin and redemption that really met the problem of sin. Salvation came from God and was not to be found in rationalistic systems of ethics or subjective mystery religions" (Cairns, pp. 45–46).

In addition to its lofty monotheism and its high code of ethics, Judaism offered hope for the future. In this respect Judaism was in direct contrast to the religions of Greece and Rome which looked back to a golden age while the Jews looked forward to the coming of the Messiah to usher in the golden age. This hope which was the unique contribution of the Jewish faith was upon more than one occasion echoed by Greek and Roman writers.

Plato expressed a longing for a world mediator who would restore peace and righteousness. The following are his words: "The perfectly righteous man, who, without doing any wrong, may assume the appearance of grossest injustice, yea, who shall be scourged, fettered, tortured, deprived of his eyesight, and after having endured all possible sufferings, fastened to a post, must restore again the beginning prototype of righteousness" (*Politia* 4:74). Such words may indicate that the messianic teachings of the Jewish Bible were familiar to Plato. To the people of the world of that day, such words gave rise to the hope of a redeemer.

Another echo of messianic hope is found in the Sibylline Oracles, a collection of poems written in Greek, which claimed to be the work of an inspired prophetess. In the Middle Ages these oracles enjoyed high authority and were often quoted by the writers of that period. One passage, which is taken from Virgil's Fourth Pastoral and which is a part of the Third Book of Sibylline Oracles, written about the first century B.C., appears to have reference to the coming of the Messiah child. This remarkable passage was translated into English by John Dryden:

> The Father banished virtue shall restore,
> And crimes shall threat the guilty world no more.
> The son shall lead the life of gods, and be
> By gods and heroes seen, and gods and heroes see.
> The jarring nations he in peace shall bind,
> And with paternal virtues rule mankind.
> Unbidden earth shall wreathing ivy bring,
> And fragrant herbs (the promises of spring),
> As her first off'rings to the infant king.

The reader of these words of the Greek poet Virgil may well be reminded of the Spanish statement: "The eyes of Virgil were the first to see the Star of Bethlehem."

Bibliography

ADAMS, J. McKEE. *Biblical Backgrounds.* Nashville: Broadman Press, 1938.

ANGUS, S. *The Environment of Early Christianity.* New York: Charles Scribner's Sons, 1915.

————. "Roman Empire," *International Standard Bible Encyclopaedia.* Vol. IV. Chicago: Howard Severance Co., 1929.

Apocrypha According to the Authorized Version, The. London: Oxford University Press, n.d.

BRUCE, F. F. *Second Thoughts on the Dead Sea Scrolls.* Grand Rapids. Wm. B. Eerdmans Publishing Co., 1964.

BURROWS, MILLAR. *More Light on the Dead Sea Scrolls.* New York: The Viking Press, 1956.

CAIRNS, EARLE E., *Christianity Through the Centuries.* Grand Rapids: Zondervan Publishing Co., 1954.

CRICHTON, JAMES. "Messiah," *International Standard Bible Encyclopaedia.* Vol. III. Chicago: Howard Severance Co., 1929.

DALMAN, GUSTOF. *Sacred Sites and Ways.* New York: The Macmillan Co., 1935.

DANA, H. E. *The New Testament World.* Nashville: Broadman Press, 1937 and 1946.

DRYDEN, JOHN. *The Poetical Works of Dryden.* (ed.) Noyes,

George R. Cambridge Edition, Boston: Houghton Mifflin Company, 1950.

ENSLIN, MORTON SCOTT. *Christian Beginnings.* New Harper Torchlight Edition. Harper & Bros., 1956.

FREE, JOSEPH P. *Archaeology and Bible History.* Wheaton: Van Kampen Press, 1950.

HENDRIKSEN, WILLIAM. *Bible Survey, A Treasure of Biblical Information.* Grand Rapids: Baker Book House, 1947.

HUFFMAN, JASPER A. *The Messianic Hope in Both Testaments.* Winona Lake: The Standard Press, 1945.

HURLBUT, JESSE LYMAN. *A Bible Atlas.* Chicago: Rand-McNally and Co., 1947.

"Judaism," *Harper's Bible Dictionary.* New York: Harper & Bros., 1952.

KITCHEN, J. HOWARD. *Holy Fields—An Introduction to the Historical Geography.* Grand Rapids: Wm. B. Eerdmans Publishing Co., 1955.

LATOURETTE, KENNETH S. *A History of the Expansion of Christianity.* Vol. I. New York: Harper & Bros., 1945.

MILLER. *Harper's Bible Dictionary,* article on "Palestine." New York: Harper and Bros., 1952.

NEWMAN, ALBERT HENRY. *A Manual of Church History.* Vol. I. Philadelphia: The American Baptist Publication Society, 1942.

NICHOL. "Dispersion," *The International Standard Bible Encyclopedia.* Vol. II.

REIKE, BO. *The New Testament Era.* Philadelphia: Fortress Press, 1968.

SACHAR, ABRAM LEON. *A History of the Jews.* 4th ed. New York: Alfred A. Knopf, 1953.

SCHULTZ, SAMUEL J. *The Old Testament Speaks.* New York: Harper & Bros., 1966.

SCHURER, EMIL. *The Jewish People in the Time of Jesus Christ.* New York: Charles Scribner's Sons, 1897 and 1953.

SMITH, GEORGE ADAM. *The Historical Geography of the Holy Land.* New York: Armstrong, 1895.

SMITH, WILBUR M. *World Crises and the Prophetic Scriptures.* Chicago: Moody Press, 1951.

TENNEY, MERRILL C. *New Testament Survey.* Grand Rapids: Wm. B. Eerdmans Publishing Co., 1953.

———. *The New Testament Times.* Grand Rapids: Wm. B. Eerdmans Publishing Co., 1965.

TERRY, MILTON S. *Biblical Hermeneutics.* Grand Rapids: Zondervan Publishing House, n.d.

TREVER, ALBERT A. *History of Ancient Civilization.* Vol. I. Harcourt-Brace Co., New York: 1936.

VON ORELLI, CONRAD. "Israel," *International Standard Bible Encyclopaedia.* Vol. III.

VOS, HOWARD F. *An Introduction to Archaeology.* Chicago: Moody Press, 1956.

WEMLEY, R. M. "Philo," *International Standard Bible Encyclopaedia.* Vol. IV.

WHISTON, WILLIAM. *The Life and Works of Flavius Josephus.* Philadelphia: Universal Book and Bible House.

ZWEMER, SAMUEL M. *The Glory of the Manger.* New York: American Tract Society, 1940.